MEMOIRS OF
THE BASTILLE

BROADWAY LIBRARY OF
EIGHTEENTH-CENTURY
FRENCH LITERATURE

THE BROADWAY LIBRARY OF EIGHTEENTH-CENTURY FRENCH LITERATURE

EDITED BY RICHARD ALDINGTON
WITH A GENERAL INTRODUCTION
BY SIR EDMUND GOSSE

DIALOGUES OF DENIS DIDEROT. Translated
by Francis Birrell

THE SOFA : A MORAL TALE. By Crébillon Fils.
Translated by Bonamy Dobrée

LETTERS OF VOLTAIRE AND FREDERICK THE GREAT.
Translated by Richard Aldington

MEMOIRS OF THE BASTILLE. By Latude and Linguet.
Translated by J. and S. F. Mills Whitham

THE PRIVATE LIFE OF THE DUC DE RICHELIEU.
Translated by F. S. Flint

MEMOIRS OF MADAME DE STAAL-DELAUNAY.
Translated by Raymond Mortimer

THE REVERIES OF A SOLITARY. By J. J. Rousseau.
Translated by John Gould Fletcher

WORKS OF JOUBERT. Translated by H. P. Collins.

MEMOIRS OF THE PRINCE DE LIGNE. Translated
by Leigh Ashton

THE SEPTEMBER MASSACRES OF 1792. Translated
by Ralph Partridge

MEMOIRS OF MADAME DE POMPADOUR. By her
waiting woman, Madame du Hausset
Translated by F. S. Flint

*SHORT STORIES BY CRÉBILLON FILS, ABBÉ DE
VOISENON, AND MONTESQUIEU.*
Translated by Mrs. Wilfrid Jackson

LETTERS OF VOLTAIRE AND MADAME DU DEFFAND.
Translated by Richard Aldington

MEMOIRS OF THE DUC DE LAUZUN.
Translated by C. K. Scott-Moncrieff

Published by
BRENTANO'S, NEW YORK

PLATE I

THE DEMOLITION OF THE BASTILLE

(From an old print)

THE BROADWAY LIBRARY
OF XVIII CENTURY FRENCH LITERATURE

MEMOIRS OF THE BASTILLE

By LATUDE AND LINGUET

Translated with an Introduction by
J. and S. F. Mills Whitham

Published by
BRENTANO'S
NEW YORK

First published in 1927.

PRINTED IN GREAT BRITAIN BY
BILLING AND SONS, LTD., GUILDFORD AND ESHER

CONTENTS

LIST OF ILLUSTRATIONS

1

INTRODUCTION

THE BASTILLE

I

HISTORY would not be a long chronicle of folly and crime if mankind had always been logical and wise, says Sir James Frazer; also that more mischief has probably been wrought in the world by honest fools in high place than by intelligent rascals. France has had a plenteous supply of one and the other in her clamourous struggles to found new Eras, to gain visionary freedom for the masses, and to impose salvation or damnation on a hunger-ridden, bewildered world; nor is clamour silenced, nor struggle of a sort ended at this day, most nations having taken their part. The Bastille, shortly before its fall, typified the embodied evils of tyranny and despotism, and became a romantic, a melodramatic symbol of the Revolution; and certainly it was the most famous, perhaps the most infamous, prison known to the so-called civilized world in its own time. Historic documents and later critical research give conflicting accounts of that imagined hell-vat steeped in human misery and inhuman woe, and the concise truth may lie midway, yet partly obscured, between blazoned extremes.

We have been told that an editor who would castrate a text on any plea of disliking the sentiment is not trustworthy and may be ripe to forge bank-notes; and in this matter of the Bastille editors did indeed confound themselves and each other in the general dark maze, searching to state and to confirm their notions, allowing feeling to outpace judgment, anger

3

to cloud logic, all more or less boisterous advocates for this or that, therefore hampered, sometimes dishonest, at the first pace in their slippery journey. Previous to the Revolution, many writers, very able of their brains and tongues, as Pepys would say, turned their exasperated attentions and their strained fancies to the Bastille; and the fearless, here and there savage, story of Latude, and the *Mémoires* of Linguet, now translated faithfully in the ensuing pages, helped to focus the minds of a vast and, as it proved in the sequel, a dangerous public on their lurid subject, one hitherto enshrouded in a dense and tantalizing mystery that gave high colour to the facts and many fictions which, eventually, were spawned prolifically. Entry to the Bastille for a peaceful sightseer had been as difficult as exit for a prisoner, and even Peter the Great, unable to secure a deviation from rule, had failed to penetrate beyond the magazine-of-arms at the bastion and prison; in addition, royal mandate enjoined that persons about to be set free from cells and dungeons must sign a declaration covenanting never by any manner of means to speak of the prison or to divulge facts concerning the prisoners, the administration, or anything familiar to him or to her by reason of their days or months or years in the Bastille: a covenant known by hearsay to all prying, thoughtful men in the years immediately preceding the Revolution, and used without stint or scruple in the business of propaganda.

On June 25th, 1760, Chevalier, major at the Bastille, wrote to Sartine, lieutenant of police, speaking apprehensively of evil rumours touching the prison, which, though in his opinion wholly false, were perilous because of repetitions spread through the kingdom in recent years. Nevertheless, no measures were taken to ventilate the mystery or to destroy legend; hence, later, Davy de Chavigné, a King's councillor, reflecting the opinion of his contemporaries, could write in all sincerity about the Bastille as a frightful monument of servitude and arbitrary power inspiring horror in all Frenchmen and soiling the annals of the nation. There were no bounds to the credulity of a restless and insatiable people, no reserves in this intense abomination of the Bastille; and the taking of the place by the revolutionary mob augmented rather than diluted the ghastly tale, a grain of fact in those tumultuous befouled days having fostered monstrous fables, such as the supposed discovery of prisoners forgotten in dungeons or sent thither to die and to rot untended. Spurious historians, verbose witlings, and others, in the days of the successful Revolution, supported these fables, and in some instances yet enlarged them; though staring facts remained in bulk sufficient to make pitiful telling by the most ingenuous and impartial worker in unbiased research. Thenceforth the Napoleonic wars and the sequent collapse of the Empire overshadowed the Bastille as a subject for pens and tongues; and, fifty years after its fall, when the Column of July marked the site where the prison had faced tempest and revolutionary storm, nothing in the shape of the monument remained actually to recall a symbol of tyranny, nor yet by inscription to give the date when the last Bastille governor capitulated.

Meanwhile the archives of the prison were hidden from sight, and the only means of establishing numerous facts lay unexplored in consequence. According to Funck-Brentano, under-librarian at the Arsenal in 1892, many huge portfolios had been stored in the prison containing its documented history from 1659, the year when this recording began; and in 1789 papers were to be counted in hundreds of thousands, comprising orders, registrations, *lettres de cachet*, chronicles, instructions, and histories relating to prisoners, governors, officers, and so forth, all sifted and collated by the archivists attached to the Bastille during the eighteenth century, representing tireless and invaluable labour on their part. Chevalier, the last major of the place, had already received orders to write a full and lucid account of the prisoners from these labelled, authentic texts. On the day of the fall, July 14th, 1789, a pillage commenced, lasting two days; and Dusaulx, one of the commissioners named by the Convention for the conserving of the Bastille archives, wrote that, when he and his colleagues reached the store-room, they found the portfolios rifled, empty, many important documents having been stolen, while the rest were strewn over the floors, scattered in the courts as far as, and into, the moats, flung thither from the towers. Later, script from the Bastille was dispersed over France and Europe, and kept in private libraries; a great mass, however, rescued and protected, stood for inspection.

"Let us collect these old title-deeds of an intolerable despotism, so to inspire horror in our descendants," a member of the Elector's Assembly cried out to his fellows, in the swollen rhetoric of the period.

La Fayette, and the Mayor of Paris, Bailly, promoted a reordering of the archives, and the Assembly of July 24th begged honourable citizens to return anything they might possess of the sort to the Town Hall. Restitutions were considerable, and the Paris Commune decided to house the documents in the Town Library, where they could be examined anew by reputable scholars. A desperate and disastrous struggle followed for the people of France, and Bastille archives were forgotten in the flame of revolution; nor did they reappear until 1840, when Ravaisson, a young librarian, rediscovered them in the Arsenal Library, where they had been transferred by Ameilhon, a cunning and ambitious fellow, in 1797, and left untouched, the said Ameilhon and his subordinates having no doubt lacked the courage and will necessary to tackle such a doughty creating of order from chaos. Ravaisson and his successors acted heroically, unsparing in effort and energy; thus, after fifty years' labour, the Bastille archives were tabulated so far as might be humanly possible subsequent to ravage by fire, water, robbery, and other inevitable mishaps.

A reasonably honest tale of the Bastille now seemed practicable, and truth might be established, if truth could or can be established in a world dazzled by illusions. Ravaisson at length published his *Archives de la Bastille* in sixteen volumes (1866 *sqq.*) ; and his nephew continued the work, volume xix. appearing in 1904; a record which may be used to check the many excessive statements in the otherwise important work *La Bastille Dévoilée*, published by Charpentier in nine parts (forming three volumes), 1789-1790.

Recent years saw the revival of an impassioned concern about the French Revolution, that fuliginous outbreak of inspiration and of insanity with its death-harvest, also its creative and fertilizing ideas, when gangrened France lay in dire need of sharp surgery. A corresponding Bastille-interest provoked much new literature, many restatements, overstressing evil and horror on the one hand, as formerly, and understating fact on the other, the most authoritative books being Funck-Brentano's *Légendes et archives de la Bastille*, Paris, 1898, a work of much value, though not infallible; and, notably, Fernand Bournon's vast addition to the *Histoire Générale de Paris*, issued by the Imprimerie Nationale, Paris, 1893. Hence, to-day, there seems to be not much left for research in the matter of material, and Carlyle's plaint that after infinite reading he could not get even so much as the plan of the building falls into past history and is memorable only inasmuch as it points to his own here and there all but insuperable difficulties, and adds to his glory.

The word Bastille in the technique of fortification hails from the fourteenth century, the thing itself from the Romans; and the Bastille of that century remained intact and almost unaltered in outward form until the day of its final surrender. The first stones were laid on April 22nd, 1370, as part of a plan to strengthen the defences of the town against English invasion, Hugues Aubriot, provost of Paris, being responsible for the work—a task completed in 1382. The main building, as it appears from the plan, oblong in shape, square on three sides, bellied slightly on the fourth, the whole having eight circular towers nearly seventy feet high, one at each angle, two of the sides showing façades of four towers almost equidistant in walls raised sixty feet, ten feet thick, surrounded by a moat twenty-five feet in depth under the drawbridges, and enclosed within defensive walls used by the patrols and adjacent to a second moat on one side encircling an elaborate bastion and small buildings auxiliary to the prison. Entry to the Bastille began from the Rue St Antoine, thus to a first court open to the public, dressed with barracks and a line of shops. This court gave access to a second, the Government Court, reached across two drawbridges side by side, one reserved for pedestrians, and always under strict observation from the neighbouring guard-houses—drawbridges now famous in history, since the real assault of July, 1789, started with the forcible and intrepid lowering of these huge iron-bound gangways. A sharp turn from this second court with its inner buildings, the governor's house and the terraces, exposed a stone alley leading to the last drawbridges and guard-rooms, the main entrance to the prison building; which likewise encompassed a major and a minor court, divided by transverse low erections constructed at a later date.

The cells were built into the towers, each tower having five stories, with dungeons bedded at the base, miasmatic black holes half-filled with water and mud when the Seine rose and the moats overflowed. The cells immediately above the dungeons had a fraction more of light, and were free from inundation, so that prisoners breathing foul damp air were at least ensured from being drowned like rats crippled in a sewer. The cells on the fifth stage ranked next to the dungeons in the inflicting of misery: the windows, or tapering slits, gave little light and less air; and summer-heat made an oven of these cells, and winterly winds an ice-bin. Each tower had a platform at the summit, united by a sort of esplanade running the entire length and breadth of the prison over the intermediary walls, where fortunate prisoners could take exercise, flanked by embrasures for guns, the building being faced with rough-hewn stone pierced by the narrow, heavily-barred windows and surmounted by an overhanging indented parapet, or embattlement. All the towers had separate names: the Corner Tower, Chapel Tower, Well Tower, so-called from their structural position; the Bertaudière and the Bazinière Towers, baptized in the name of well-known prisoners walled therein; the Treasure Tower, one-time used as a store for money and jewels. The seventh, the County Tower, honoured a feudal dignity of Paris; and the eighth, Liberty Tower, may have been christened by a bitter ironist, or, more likely, defined the quarters of prisoners relatively blessed and allowed freedom of a kind within the outer walls of the gaol.

The monumental Bastille clock, known to the world from Linguet's description, frowned on the major court of the prison: therefore prisoners who were not allowed to take exercise on the platforms overlooking the city, and could see no more than a scrap of sky enframed by grey stone as they trudged round and about the dreary echoing quad like so many wretched animals in a stone cage, were able to watch the passing of time and to shudder at sinister decorations encircling the great dial. D'Argenson, one of the Marquise de Pompadour's many enemies, seems to have been the originator of this ferocious affair, he having commissioned Quillet, a Parisian clockmaker, to devise a work suggested by him, begun in 1763 and finished two years later; for which Quillet received high pay, and an inducement each year to keep order in the machinery of his cynical masterpiece. However, after the publication and the diffused popularity of Linguet's *Mémoires*, including his caustic animadversions on the Bastille clock, M. de Breteuil, a King's minister indirectly affined to the Bastille, ordered that the outrageous decorative chains should be removed from the thing forthwith. This was done; and the two figures, male and female, modelled to represent enslavement, fell at last to the plunder of architect Palloy, the official demolisher of the Bastille soon after its capitulation.

From the foregoing essentially brief account, a patient reader may be able partly to imagine the Bastille as it shadowed the Rue St Antoine at the end of the fourteenth century, and as it appeared to the crowd in 1789.

II

The Bastille, built as a fortress, a defended and supposed invulnerable town-entrance, was not immediately used as a prison; and the story that Hugues Aubriot, responsible for the original construction, loved the Jews, adopted their faith, suffered the repressive power of the Bishop, and spent the rest of his days walled by his own work, is apocryphal; yet records show that prisoners were sent to the Bastille as early as 1403,

two sorcerers, after promising and failing to cure
Charles VI of madness, having gained the ambiguous
distinction of heading the punitive list. Subsequently,
the English were temporary masters of the Bastille,
which served, among other functions, as a prison
during their occupation; but the place did not acquire
its sombre true character until about the second half
of the fifteenth century, when Louis XI, the first of
the absolute French kings, used it for the time being
as a State prison.

Louis, with his black caps and leaden virgins,
amused and instructed himself in a study of prisons
and the devising of games for the direct and indirect
torment of perverse citizens. He is said to have
clapped the D'Armagnac princes in Bastille dungeons
hollowed at the centre by inverted stone cones, from
which they could not clamber and where, hemmed in,
unable to find rest or footing, they lived, or rather died
by slow degrees, released only twice a week so that
they might be flogged in view of the governor, and
every three months to have teeth wrenched from their
jaws before they were flung again into the stone
coffins. Certainly the ingenious and occasionally
vindictive Louis must be held responsible for the
celebrated iron cages used throughout his reign,
though perhaps not thenceforth, at the Bastille, and
designed actually by the Bishop of Verdun; who, says
Commines in his *Mémoires*, was the first to be thus
caged, having fourteen years—twelve years, Bournon
writes—in which to admire and to suffer his finished
work. Louis, yet exercising his peculiar genius, had
a special and a nefarious system of leg and body irons,
supplemented by chains weighted with iron balls;
also collars to grind holes in the neck of a prisoner,
pillories to cramp him almost to extinction, and other
iron tricks of the sort, all stored for use at the Bastille.
Prisoners were put to the Question, Ordinary and

Extraordinary, in accord with their power to endure grades of torture by " Boot " and torture by " Water." Readers of Scott's *Old Mortality* will recall the horror of the one device: the other consisted in chaining a victim to the floor and swelling him with water forced down his throat, four separate drenches being ordinary torture, eight extraordinary; nor was this invariably considered enough in the matter of agony: for example, in 1663, Davot, a priest guilty of sacrilege and committed to the Bastille, stood condemned " to make *amende honorable* in front of the principal door of Notre Dame, to be hung and strangled on a gallows . . . his dead body cast into the flames and his ashes scattered to the winds; the said Davot first of all to suffer the Ordinary and the Extraordinary Question, to force the truth from his mouth." Ravaisson, giving record of a torturing, among many similar in form, quotes from a *procès-verbal* dated 1691: a canon of Beauvais, named Foy, imprisoned for plotting against Louis XIV, fell to the torturer, and, placed on the *sellette de la question*, and after being tied by the arms, had his hose and shoes removed in preparation for the dreadful boot. He failed to give the answers expected from him in confession, and the torture began. He screamed out that he was dying; and again, and yet again under increased sufferings; so until the doctor intervened, determined to save the life of the ambitious canon; who was revived with wine, haled anew to his cell, and left all but dead on his mattress. This kind of thing occurred at the Bastille until about 1720, when maybe humanity sickened at itself.

In the meantime, secrecy and mystery had been maintained rigidly in all things affecting the prison, as may be seen in a characteristic letter from Catherine de Medici to Montmorency, her cousin. She writes that a prisoner intended for the Bastille shall be sent from Rouen to Paris, and locked up in such fashion

that no one may know of it, or have any means of
discovering his whereabouts. /Thus, in those days
and through the ages, men and women vanished from
their families and associates as completely as if they
had been dissolved into air and were heard of no more;
and several were at laſt buried dead in Baſtille earth
after burial alive in a Baſtille cell, becoming duſt,
and with nothing to mark their graves, nothing in or
out of the prison to announce to their fellows that
such ſtricken creatures had been or had ceased to be.
Habeas corpus is comparatively a modern luxury in
France.

The real or supposed crimes of Baſtille prisoners
were evidently as varied as the methods of treatment
to which culprits were subjeɗted; and in the sixteenth
century the whole of the *Parlement* followed its chiefs
to the prison, where many of the members were duly
entombed. L'Eſtoile tells the ſtory, and describes
the march through crowded vociferous streets when,
as he says, by a judgment of God, the firſt court of
Europe allowed itself to be led in triumph and imprisoned; and these dignitaries were kept in the Baſtille,
treated roughly and sometimes brutally, until one by
one, through this means or that, they succeeded in
making peace with despotism and so returned to their
homes, saddened no doubt, and perhaps more mature
in wisdom. Henry IV used the Baſtille specifically
as a treasure-house, and Biron ſtands out as the moſt
diſtinguished of the few prisoners in that reign, he
having conspired, wishful to sell the French crown to
Spain. The Biron family had enough influence to
prevent his publiċ execution after the death sentence
and the confiscation of his property; accordingly the
officials dressed a scaffold in a corner of the prisoners'
court; where Biron wept and pleaded and ſtruggled
as the attendants pinioned him and bandaged his eyes.
Finally the executioner lopped off Biron's head at one

stroke, with much dexterity, says report, and whilst the wretched fellow continued to mutter his prayers.

By the time Louis XIII, and Richelieu, ruled France, the Bastille had become a State prison exclusively, differing from others built for common or ordinary criminals, except when a malefactor chanced to be great in his family or too powerful in prestige and influence to be herded with more vulgar creatures; and it remained a State prison until its fall. The first discoverable list of prisoners is dated 1643, giving the names and, in most entries, the crimes: fifty-three in all, overcrowding the place. There are several suspected of evil designs against the Cardinal; conspirators intriguing to undermine the throne; an " extravagant priest "; and forgers, assassins, lunatics, " wicked devils," and so on. A second list, 1661, is yet more explicit and varied, and here figures a crazy vicar who had been running the roads and shouting to excite sedition; another who tormented the King by calling him " gossip " (*compère*); M. de Bernier, wicked to his mother and his brothers, and " wanting to kill everybody "; others who disliked the Duke of Orleans or Mazarin; a bigamist; priests guilty of impiety; " gazetteers " who found no one eager to vindicate their false news, or openly to respect writings intended to impugn the surety of the State and the dignity of the Government. Later, as Bournon remarks, these penurious, vain fellows with their scurrilous pens and satirical couplets were too numerous to be imprisoned in the Bastille, such treatment being reserved for writers who, by their independence and their philosophy, rendered themselves suspicious to authority. Yet further lists include deserters from the army, spies, booksellers making money out of sedition or obscenity, searchers for the philosopher's stone, heretics, a sodomist; and a Scotch Jacobite who lived for thirty-four years in the Bastille, killed a turnkey with an iron bar, and thereafter had his meals served to him through an aperture in the door.

Under Louis XIV all and any means were used to repress heresies, and, by analogy, religious maniacs who dealt in mircaulous cures, prophecy, convulsions; and many of these besotted or enraptured fanatics suffered excessive punishment designed to lead them to confession and the Faith—punishments futile as a rule, often ending in natural, or unnatural, death. Later, the Bastille gorged itself with groups of prisoners, mostly women, guilty of a hitherto sparsely known crime especially heinous and alarming. A strange epidemic of poisoning had spread over Paris and elsewhere like a plague; to say truth, a frenzy, first noticed in 1673 when parish priests, horrified by tales heard in confession and growing in number steadily, considered themselves bound as good citizens, if not as Holy Fathers, to inform the lieutenant of police. Ravaisson, in his study of this pest, suggests that the Fronde, having crowded men on battlefields, gave unexpected freedom and opportunity to women, whose husbands, returning from the wars and brutalized by slaughter and lust, retaliated viciously and were there-fore regarded by their suffering wives as fair game for reprisals; in addition, communication with Spain had infected French people with romantic notions, jealousies, vendettas, and, licence being rampant and morality in rags, fidelity to the marriage-bed became old-fashioned and insipid. No doubt witchcraft had been invoked, since obscure rites and a foul ritual were used by women anxious and determined to poison their husbands: many of these seeming harpies, skilled in treachery and cunning, and by means protracted or brief, contrived to make their victims swallow or breathe arsenic. Special laws were enacted to eradicate the evil; years were involved in the stern process; and accounts remain to-day to puzzle the wits of students who would fathom the inscrutable psychology of perversions and inhuman follies, and probe to the quick of the devil-worship ulcer.

Imprisonments by *lettres-de-cachet* seem to have been common at all times in the gloomy history of the Bastille, and any citizen of rank or a noble at court might overtly or by devious ways succeed in having a troublesome relative silenced for a time, and with the utmost reliable secrecy, or could rid himself of an enemy less powerful than he. The formula of these sealed letters seldom varied in character—for example:

" To M. de Launey, governor of my château de la Bastille, or, in his absence, to whosoever may be in command.

" M. de Launey, I send this letter to instruct you to receive in my château de la Bastille the said Danry, surgeon's assistant, and Bengué, apothecary's assistant, and to detain them until a new order from me. Herein I pray God to keep you, M. de Launey, and to guard you. Written at Marly, May 1st, 1749.

" LOUIS."

Danry is the famous Latude.

Sedition is another crime frequent in the annals of the Bastille, those who were convicted of such practices, or, more often, only suspected, being whisked off without warning, and always mysteriously—since mystery and the Bastille were correlative terms—to the old fortress, the lists including all ranks from inn-keepers and pedlars to aristocrats and statesmen. Linguet is to be ranked in this category; and Latude, indirectly. Of all Bastille prisoners, however, none is so notorious, in legend, as the " Man in the Iron Mask "; none so alluring as a tale in the many tales of the prison with its one-time nearly impenetrable veil to shield it from searching inquisition. The unknown prisoner, incidentally, wore a black velvet mask, not

an iron contrivance with steel articulations, wherefore
he might eat and, presumably, blow his caged nose.

He entered the Bastille on September 18th, 1698,
at three o'clock in the afternoon, accompanied by
Saint-Mars, formerly his gaoler elsewhere, and now
about to take charge of the prison as governor; and
here the masked man remained till his death in 1703.
His name does not figure on the prison register, where
he is cited as one obliged always to carry a mask, nor
must anyone be permitted to see or to hear him, except
the governor and the major of the prison; and, under
the heading Motives of Detention, his crime is said
to be no more known than his name. Michelet wrote
that the puzzle of the " Man in the Iron Mask " would
probably remain for ever darkly obscure; whereas
Funck-Brentano, in his *Légendes de la Bastille*, declares
that he has solved the riddle, and proceeds to unfold
it in detail, after stating that for two centuries no
figure so intrigued the public, and that books written
on the subject would cram a library. Voltaire, in
his well-known *Siècle de Louis XIV*, mentions the
iron mask, and says the prisoner lay under the death
penalty if he removed it; and, in the second edition of
Questions sur l'Encyclopédie, the vigorous old giant
adds that the man was half-brother to Louis XIV, son
to Mazarin and Anne of Austria, and, much more
significantly, the elder of the two. This is the most
famous declaration in what might be called the innumerable historical fables concerning the " Man in
the Iron Mask," as Dumas' *Vicomte de Bragelonne* is
the most famous in fiction.

Actually, says Funck-Brentano after patient and
praiseworthy research, the man was Mattioli, Secretary
of State to the Duke of Mantua, born at Bologna on
December 1st, 1640, distinguished in his family,
brilliant in his career as a youth and later as a University professor; and he managed to establish himself

2

at Mantua, confidant first to Charles III, then to
Charles IV. The Abbé d'Estrades, French Ambassador to the Venetian Republic at this period, a
shrewd, cunning fellow with a tutored instinct for
intrigue, met Mattioli, and, divining the young states-
man's particular and kindred genius, secured his help
in furthering the projects of the French Court in the
plaguy matter of Casal, the township coveted by the
King whence, with Pignerol, acquired by Louis XIV,
France could dominate Upper Italy and keep the Court
of Turin under control. In 1678 Louis wrote express-
ing his thanks to Mattioli, whom he invited to Paris;
where, on December 8th of that year, an act was signed
by which the Duke of Mantua would receive 100,000
crowns in exchange for Casal. Louis gave Mattioli
a valuable diamond and 100 double-louis for his
momentous service. All seemed well. About two
months later, however, the Courts of Vienna, Madrid,
Turin, and the Venetian Republic heard of the secret,
sly transaction; and they were excited and angered.
Mattioli had betrayed his master Charles, together with
Louis, his benefactor. The envoy appointed by the
French to exchange the ratifications was arrested
promptly; Louis raged in his indignation against the
deception of others; and d'Estrades, by way of requital
on behalf of his master, proposed that Mattioli should
be abducted with all possible speed, in despite of inter-
national law, rather than that such a subtle and cynical
villain might be allowed to crow in triumph. Louis
agreed: hence, on May 2nd, 1679, Mattioli, inveigled
by d'Estrades, found himself shut in the fortress at
Pignerol soon after noon, and in charge of Saint-Mars.
Fifteen years later, Saint-Mars transferred his
prisoner to the Isles of Sainte-Marguerite, thence
eventually to the Bastille; where Mattioli, withered and
parched, thought of himself and the favour of princes,
and died at last from illness, also probably from misery

and chagrin; nor is there any record to show that his friends in Italy knew the facts; for the political importance of hiding the circumstance of his abduction had necessarily been great.

Funck-Brentano suggests that Mattioli received lenient, even generous, treatment at the Bastille; which may or may not be true; though documentary evidence proves that many prisoners were in fact highly privileged and lived more or less luxuriously, often at the expense of their respective captors. Assuredly the lists of administrative officers demonstrate that ample provisions were made for the upkeep of health and order. There was the governor; a deputy-governor; a major, bound each day to report current prison facts to the lieutenant of police; an engineer, responsible for the buildings; a surgeon in residence, and a doctor living in private and always at command; a midwife, whose functions were rarely exercised; a secretary for the archives; a chaplain, a confessor, and two honorary ecclesiastical gentlemen; a police commissioner, and four turnkeys. Meanwhile, always there were soldiers and officers in garrison; forty-seven men in all at the start of the eighteenth century, commanded by the governor and the major. Louis XV created a new company of pensioners, garrisoned at the Bastille, comprising a captain, a sub-captain, their lieutenants, four sergeants, four corporals, four lance-corporals, sixty-eight fusiliers, and two drummers. The King's reasons for assigning pensioners to guard-work are not clear; and unquestionably these odd and sometimes crippled soldiers were inept for such a task, nor were the appointments considered enviable; which perhaps accounts in degree for the tepid defence of the Bastille on the part of almost everybody immediately concerned ere its fall. The company, lodged in the barracks of the forecourt, had nothing to do with the cells, these being left strictly to the turnkeys; and the pensioners could at least make a brave show when prisoners arrived under escort, or court officials were received and honoured at the drawbridges.

Such was the system of administration at the Bastille in 1789; such was the size of the garrison until a few weeks before the assault, when the heads of Government, forecasting possible danger, raised the men's pay, made pretence of reorganizing the artillery, sent a lieutenant and over forty men to strengthen the defences, and then waited with suspicion and disquiet to see what might happen, encouraging themselves and each other, assuming the place must be impregnable, the forces reliable, and that Parisian mobs were too ragged and demagogues too contradictory ever to be a lively peril to the nation. Revolution, seemingly, could be only a dream, a nightmare for fanatics; and riots hitherto had been suppressed and were mostly forgotten. In the meantime, only seven prisoners lay at the Bastille, including two lunatics, the Marquis de Sade having been sent to Charenton, an asylum, on July 4th, ten days before the fall, and after an imprisonment of several years as punishment for his perversions and mania; otherwise this intractable gentleman also might have been paraded in the streets on July 15th, and acclaimed and fondled as a hero because he too had suffered in the thrice-cursed prison, now in the hands of the people and shortly to be wiped out as if it were a pestilential dark blot on French soil, a disgrace to mankind, a horror to the gods, and especially to angels of Liberty, of which there were supposed to be many on wing and afoot in and about Paris at that time.

III

Sterne wished for readers who would give up the reins of their imaginations and place them into the hands of the author; and indubitably there have been many authors with like earnest hopes in the darksome matter of the assault on and the fall of the Bastille. The literal full story is not easily disentangled from conjecture; and a confusion of tongues or pens beclouds the subject and plagues the reader. "What man can walk accurately by the law of truth for one day?" Carlyle wrote, he too having had to wade and search through much vacant, sonorous prose concerning things historical and fabulous. Bournon, Funck-Brentano, and several would-be scrupulous writers of sound erudition and good sense, suggest directly or otherwise that the issue in the Rue St Antoine on July 14th, 1789, was not at all compatible with the simplicity and honesty of the design; and though other skilled French chroniclers might argue, after Flaubert, that to understand Nature it is necessary to be as calm as Nature, they do not inevitably follow precept. Thus the taking of the Bastille has been described on the one hand as if it were an horrific doomsday leading to a new earth and heaven; and, on the other, disparaged into something not unlike a vulgar scuffle started unintentionally by a respectable group of citizens anxious to get arms, so to protect their properties from roving bedraggled bands of hungered brigands.

"After us, the deluge," Madame de Pompadour had said to her lover, Louis XV, misquoting him; and July 14th was perchance the first wave of that deluge, though subterraneous tides had ebbed and flowed for years previously, indeed for ages. Madame de Pompadour's honourable maid, Madame du Hausset, quotes in her *Mémoires* from an anonymous letter sent to the King: a long and pregnant epistle censuring the times and loaded with warnings.   A day would come, the writer continued, when the People might awaken; and he prayed the King to take command of his State, governing firmly, and to give the lie to critics who insisted that His Highness thought only of his women, rejoiced only with rakes and titled rascals, and assumed that such capers were the cherished privilege of Royalty.   Had the anonymous writer been discovered, he would have passed promptly and secretly to the Bastille; but he was not discovered, nor, apparently, could the King gather any unequivocal sense from the letter: therefore Louis XV's grandson, suffering for his sire, also for himself, had to pay with his head, and France with much of its best, and some of its worst, blood; and the Bastille became a ruin.

There had been sundry attacks on the Bastille in its long history; and always the governor was forced to make terms, or to capitulate without them.   During the twenty years of strife and broils at the commencement of the fifteenth century, Bastille-possession and possession of the city were supposed to be identical. In 1413 D'Epernon and his men, who belonged to the Burgundian party, were besieged at the Bastille, and, since there were 24,000 resolute fellows at the gates, surrendered.   Five years later the Armagnacs held the place, were cornered by the Burgundians; and they too capitulated.   When the English occupied Paris, John Falstofe, or Falstaff, governed the Bastille in the name of Henry V: and what a larding of Bastille floors and a swallowing of purloined sack must have followed had the said Falstofe been Shakespeare's fat knight!   The English troops retired into the Bastille, previous to evacuation of the city and a withdrawal to Rouen when the seceding Burgundians, allied now to the French, entered Paris.   The prison-fortress was besieged once more during the religious wars of the sixteenth century, and occupied by Condé;

and in 1594 again it surrendered, this time to the
forces of Henry IV.   In 1649, when the Fronde had
armed itself in revolt, Parisians with cannon menaced
the Bastille, and the governor, Tremblay, after refusing
at first to be bought out, decided to walk out in haste,
alarmed by a few shots from the crowd; and he gave
up the keys, and his office, and so departs in shame
from history.   In 1709, a year of great distress and
misery, one foreshadowing the Revolution, the populace endangered the Bastille, making preparation for
attack; but precautions taken in the matter of defensive
armament chilled the temper of the crowd, and the
event, so to speak, was postponed for eighty years; by
which time France, thanks among numerous factors
to Kings and Kings' whores, to knaves and fools in
and out of office, had reached a razor-edge of bank-
ruptcy, and the Government, unable to stem disaster,
tottered, about to collapse.

Authority at this time had already engaged itself in
considering the demolition of the Bastille, now nearly
obsolete, and expensive as a means of defence and as
a State prison; nevertheless the eight towers and the
dense walls remained, a sinister and a symbolic figure,
a crystallization, in the view of Parisians and of French
people.   Revolutionary impulses were at work, fermenting, about to swell and to overflow.   Famine
confronted the urban population, crops having failed
in many districts, corn being fatally scarce, food a
rare luxury to impoverished thousands.   These woeful
facts were ascribed by disingenuous and insidious
orators to the plottings of base aristocrats, and accepted
as such by hungering poor creatures prone to believe
almost anything against tyranny, and nearly ripe to
do anything in their need and a demented hope for
the realization of trumpeted freedom.

Louis XVI, weak and will-less, alternated endlessly
between extremes, now favouring and promoting

reforms, anon recoiling, intimidated by his ministers, surrounded by parasites, Court flunkeys, busybodies; tricked, deceived, applauded, defeated, and always bewildered. He had been forced to consent to the States General; which, by way of the Third Estate, the Commons, managed to shape itself into a National Assembly after much futile endeavour; for the Nobles, the Clergy and the Deputies, three groups forming the States General, divided and hostile, were impotent as a governing body. Hence eventually the Deputies took their own way, named their own president, and vowed that they themselves were the Nation. They appointed committees for this and that, devised fruitless acts in the panting effort to save France from starvation, and from financial and other imminent wreckage; and they were braced to ignore the King, if needful, and to despise the Court. On June 20th they found their assembly-room, commandeered by royal order, full of soldiers; for the King had proclaimed a Royal Séance, to be held in a few days, preparations were imperative, workmen already busy under escort of troops. The deputies, frustrated for the moment, yet recalcitrant, betook themselves with their grievances to a covered tennis court, and elected to pursue business there, repeating oaths of fidelity to their principles, determined to be a governing National Assembly in face of Kings and Nobles, and muskets piled for use. They represented the People, and, as they asseverated flamboyantly, were ready to die for the People in the attempt to give Frenchmen something better than meal-husks and boiled grass. At the Royal Séance, the King decreed that " the three orders shall vote separately "; soon after, however, and when most of the Clergy had joined the Commons, he begged the Nobles to oblige him by submission. Thus the Third Estate triumphed.

Notwithstanding, regiments were being moved

mysteriously to and fro across Paris, and taxes were imposed for their support, the capital having resolved itself into a state of siege. Restive French Guards, imprisoned, were liberated by shouting mobs. Crowds of patriots, as they named themselves, parading and acclaiming a bust of the minister Necker, now in disgrace and about to go into retirement, were charged and maimed by dragoons, and foreign troops used to supplement, or to supplant, a wavering French soldiery already stained deeply by the general misery and mistrust.

Cannon lumbered in the streets of Paris and on the highways thither; Broglie, the war lord, had his head-quarters at Versailles, and, he fancied, was as ready as the National Assembly to do his particular business, to riddle such assemblies and to restore order with grape-shot; and no doubt the valiant Broglie would have used his grape-shot, had the troops remained staunch. Unfortunately for him, the French Guards, the best regiment of the line, simmered in revolt; additional squads were disposed to drink to the King and to the Nation with the people, and otherwise to let the lave go by: and Broglies are barren, though noisy, when grape-shot cannot get itself into cannon and out again by fire.

Such would seem to have been the plight of Paris and its citizens early in July; and on Sunday the 12th the streets were strewn with further proclamations ordering householders to stay within doors, so to abstain from collecting. The ill-fated, ardent Camille Desmoulins, and other grandiose patriots, belaboured the crowds, who did *not* stay at home on that thunder-some day; and soon a cry " To Arms!" spread broad-cast from the Palais Royal, the storm-centre, and grew in fever, acting like sparks to powder. Paris, now hysterical, roused itself to action: how, where, why, appears to have been no immediate concern of anyone in the welter of emotion that galvanized the torpid into movement and the rebellious to fury.

No doubt a large body of reasonable worthy citizens, imagining that government had fallen to rags and so they must protect themselves, did, in fact, want arms solely to defend their own goods, and had no thought of revolution; others took advantage of the mesmeric cry, foreseeing possibilities, eager to abet the destruction of what to them was a despotism cruel and blind; others again saw chance of loot; and many cried for arms because their neighbours cried for arms. Whatever the dominant motive, records show that within a few hours a vast yelling mob searched high and low for arms. The Town Council had evaporated, discreetly and with speed, and were thenceforth negligible; Versailles hung suspended, frightened or sceptical or indifferent, certainly ineffective, while commanders in different parts of the city sent couriers for orders and could not extract answer from anyone; a Provisional Municipality, inspired by the Assembly of Electors then sitting in Paris, had formed itself, and began to enrol a Parisian Militia, upholding the call for arms, seeking to direct and to control it.

On the 13th the uproar had veritably become a madness. Shops were shut and barricaded, streets swarmed with insurgents, women were sewing tri-colour cockades; meanwhile, to add to the direful hullabaloo, bells were clanging in all the steeples and towers; for it would seem, in the history of France, that church-bells clattered without respite were an unshunnable necessity on all and every occasion of tumult. The Provisional Municipality slaved at its self-appointed task, distributing arms, calling for more; and subsidiary district groups did likewise. Repositories were forced and rifled, prisons broken; deserters from the troops had joined marauding bands; and French Guards, ordered to take position, refused in a body, and gave themselves to insurrection, together with their arms and cannon.

On the morning of the Fourteenth the cry had reached a vertex, and the crowd surged to the Hôtel des Invalides, where 28,000 muskets and 124 cannon were housed in the cellars. De Sombreuil, the governor, afraid that his guard could not be trusted to resist vigorously, tried to parley with the crowd and failed. Gates were smashed, walls scaled, the cellars ransacked. Now the shout rose: " To the Bastille!" and in a brief time the roads surrounding the Invalides were deserted and the Rue St Antoine had become the electric centre of the drama.

De Launey, the predestined, governor of the Bastille, had received royal orders to hold the fortress and prison with his pensioners and the Swiss reinforcements sent recently; and he had food-provision for one day, and only for one day; but there were cannon on the parapets, already charged and pointed, and de Launey, indomitable in his age, believed he was prepared to fire his own powder-magazine and send himself and the Bastille sky-high rather than to surrender. The Municipality, earnest to prevent slaughter and aware of the scene in the Rue St Antoine, dispatched representatives to de Launey, beseeching him to withdraw his cannon from the embrasures and to refrain from hostile act, assuring him that the crowd were not conspiring to attack him or to demolish his Bastille, exercised as they were for their own protection. These representatives were received courteously by the hapless governor, refused offers of lunch, and departed in a seemly fashion after being informed that the cannon would be withdrawn.

Soon after, a second deputation, led by advocate Thuriot, arrived at the drawbridges, though apparently they were sent by the householders of the district and did not officially represent municipal authority.

Thuriot, wordy in argument, high and insolent when roused, insisted on a right of entry, and de Launey consented, reluctant this time. He led Thuriot and his fellows to the parapets, where they could see the cannon, displaced now, a few feet out of position, though charged, facing the city. Thuriot expressed his dissatisfaction, probably in the name of the Nation and Patriotism, the usual formula; but de Launey refused to do more, and announced his intention of blowing the Bastille to atoms if provocation did not cease. Thuriot descended, a grim little gentleman, very determined, harangued the garrison once more in the name of national honour and what not, heard from them that they would not fire unless they were attacked; and he returned to the crowd—a crowd beginning to sway ominously, gathering momentum from its own hysteria, fast becoming excessively dangerous.

Thuriot reported at the Town Hall; and the Municipality, yet striving manfully to curb evil and to maintain a factitious order, sent another deputation to de Launey, urging him to give whatever arms he might have to the Commune, thus to aid public defence, arguing that they were at the head of the Parisian Militia, advising him to join with them and to take their men as part of his defensive guard. De Launey, loyal to his duty, refused; whereupon the attack commenced, led by would-be heroes already inflamed and confident after the amazing success at the Invalides.

The stormers passed from the first to the second court and confronted the raised drawbridges; and whether firing by the garrison had or had not started at this pinch may be doubtful: anyhow, it was brisk enough presently. Two daring fellows clambered to the roof of the guard-house next to the drawbridges, and smote the chains with hatchets until the gangways fell. The besiegers thronged into the inner court,

PLATE II

THE STORMING OF THE BASTILLE

[face p. 28

and faced the last entrance to the prison, this too, with
its drawbridges raised.   A hail of shot came incessantly
from loopholes in the Bastille walls; and numerous
musketeers filling the upper windows of houses in the
vicinity of the prison returned the fire, helped by guns
in the court, and cannon; all without effect on walls
ten feet thick. A young woman, caught in the act of   *Imp*
escape, and at once and erroneously named daughter
to de Launey by the susceptible mob, fell to a murderous group and was dragged to the fore, about to be
burned alive if the governor refused to capitulate.
Others, less murderous, rescued her and smuggled
her into safety.   De Launey, expecting and longing
for help from the painfully inert Broglie with his
unshootable grape-shot, could not further doubt his
extreme jeopardy, a troop of hussars, scared by the
scene or in sympathy with the stormers, having arrived
and dispersed and vanished, they too useless.

About three o'clock a final deputation came from
the Town Hall, and, though de Launey seems to have
shown a white flag on the walls, after ordering his men
to display themselves with arms reversed, the Swiss,
below, continued to make bloody havoc in the crowd;
and the deputation likewise dispersed and vanished,
this time at peril of their lives.   Three carts laden with
straw were hauled forward and kindled, almost choked
the men attending them, and increased the huddle by
half blinding the rest; and, at this pass, apparently, the
one solitary shot from Bastille cannon that day added
to the maiming of the besiegers and redoubled their
rage.   Cannon were being placed by French Guards
affined to the vaunted Commune; and de Launey,
forsaken by authority, uncertain of his men, trapped,
dismayed, baffled, nearly beaten, went down to the
magazine, intent to make fact of his threat, preferring,
as he said to his officers, to be scattered with his Bastille
rather than to have his throat cut by the populace.

His men withheld him, saved the place from destruction that day, and de Launey from a death honourable and even merciful in relation to the fate reserved for him before nightfall.

White flags were brandished anew; the garrison ceased fire immediately, the attackers half an hour later, they being too overwrought and lustful to imagine that victory drew near. Then they demanded the instant lowering of the drawbridge, meaning to penetrate into the prison, satisfied with nothing less. De Launey parleyed with them from a loophole, admitting defeat if he and his men might be allowed to march from the place " with the honours of war," in his pathetic phrase. No one would hear him, so he passed a paper through the loophole, having written that he had great store of powder and would shatter the place and the garrison if the people refused to accept his capitulation. A plank was laid across the moat, and a bold fellow, approaching to take the paper, lost his balance, fell, and broke his neck. A second, more cautious and skilful, succeeded. Élie, a captain on half-pay, who had led the assault, accepted de Launey's submission and terms, on his faith of an officer, as he said. De Launey wished to have a ratification from the Town Hall, but the crowd would not wait; consequently the drawbridges were lowered. The Bastille had fallen.

The end of the tale makes dreadful reading. Neither Élie nor any men alive at that five o'clock hour were competent to shackle the anger of the miscellaneous victors, nor to redeem a pledge. The crowd had lost eighty-three dead, fifteen wounded mortally, sixty disabled; and others were drunk with their own savagery. Men were firing on each other, killing friends in the insane need to kill enemies. De Launey, discovered as he was about to end his days with his sword-cane, looking to right and left like an old grey cornered

badger, appealed to Élie; who, with an escort, struggled
to help the poor creature, set off with him to the Town
Hall, waving the capitulation paper in effort to appease
the crowd. Élie and his friends were overthrown;
and de Launey, stabbed like a Cæsar, torn, blinded
with his own blood, pleaded for a last and a kindly
stroke; and his head stuck on a pike soon led the
procession. Other officers were massacred at once,
or hanged " on the lantern " subsequently; and the
entire squad might have shared a like fate during that
triumphant bedlam-hour. The French Guards, however, managed at last to protect the survivors, and the
crowd, glutted momentarily and maybe in a quick
reaction, acclaimed the Bastille garrison, offered re-
freshments to them, followed them cheering to the
barracks of the Guard. Simultaneously, the Bastille
was ransacked and pillaged in every nook and crevice,
the seven prisoners were released and worshipped;
and had there been enough power in the mob, the very
walls of the ancient fortress might have been torn
down and the foundations uprooted; work reserved for
a later, though not distant, date.

Most accounts of these July 14th events end, as
this account shall end, with the same dramatic curtain,
history having provided a fact of the sort unsurpassed
by art; especially so in view of the tragedies brewing.

On the night of that baneful day the Duke de Lian-
court entered the royal apartments at Versailles; and,
having awakened Louis XVI, he recorded the scene
in the Rue St Antoine.

" Then it is a revolt ? " the King said.

" Sire, it is not a revolt.   It is a Revolution."

LATUDE

HENRI MASERS DE LATUDE

INTRODUCTION

ARTISTS romantic and otherwise are, in the main, the product of their time, but woe to them, as someone wrote, if they become the pupils of their time; and the astonishing, indeed the occasionally astounding, subject of this Introduction was incontrovertibly the product of his time, and he knew more of woe than most men. He is yet dignified by the false name of Masers de Latude, having learned while in the Bastille of Henri Vissec de la Tude's death at the wars, electing straightway to become the son of that gallant officer; and he appropriated the family. Thus all reference in the following Memoirs to the prisoner's sire must be considered fanciful. Jean Henri is the true name; and, in the spread and progress of his adventures, and his miseries, he became Danry, Daury, Danger, Jédor, and finally Latude; and, since he was fastidious in these matters and succeeded in imposing a chosen name on his contemporaries, Latude he shall be in this short account of his days: a man odd and slippery in his genius, and with as much life-force pulsing through his little finger as commonly hives in the whole carcase of an ordinary peaceful citizen. Bournon declares that the tale of Latude, together with the *Mémoires* of Linguet, consummated the public loathing and fear of the Bastille, and brought about its fall: an excessive statement, perhaps, yet not conspicuously wide of the whole truth, though Latude, in his customary headlong fashion, and excluding Linguet, would have agreed heartily with Bournon. An old

engraving of the celebrated prisoner shows him in
his hoary years with his equally celebrated rope-
ladders and the machinery of escape; a portly fellow,
serene now, also intense, his great eyes full of compassion, his mouth drawn in a humoursome, a slightly
derisive, smile, his right arm uplifted and pointing to
the background; where creatures like automatic dolls
are at work demolishing a Baſtille tower. The
inscription runs: " HENRI MASERS DE LATUDE. Detained during 35 years in various State prisons.
Taught by his misfortunes and his captivity how to
foil the attempts and the anger of tyrants, he showed
Frenchmen that true courage can conquer liberty."
The phrasing, the attitude of the figure and the para-
phernalia encompassing it, are monumentally charac-
teriſtic of Latude.

His faults were innumerable, his idiosyncrasies
incalculable, and his tempeſtuous vanity eclipsed moſt
things of the sort before and after his time; he had a
voice of thunder, one of his captors wrote, which could
be heard all through, and outside, the Baſtille, and
Latude used it frequently; his inflammable imagination tolerated no bounds, and doubtless he believed
many of his own startling, elaborate, and sometimes
infantile, fiĉtions; and his manias were profuse, waxing
as his years waned.   Latude, however, groped through
human misery and torment to its hard unyielding dark
core, nor was his manhood crushed; in short, his
virtues largely redeem his vices, and give him a notable
place in the ſtory.   He reminds one here and there of
Casanova, or of the unfortunate and resolute Baron
Trenck; in addition, there were ſtreaks of Caglioſtro
in him, likewise a vivid dash of Meredith's Richmond-
Roy; and his *Mémoires* may be read, relished, and
shelved beside Cellini's.

Thierry, Latude's firſt editor, believed in him without
a peradventure, and reverenced him because of his

PLATE III

HENRI MASERS DE LATUDE

[*face p. 36*

protracted, deep suffering. Barrière—from whose edition this translation is made—perhaps more dubious and sophisticated than Thierry, gave no biographical account of the man, allowing the *Mémoires* to tell their own at times appalling story. Funck-Brentano, following Ravaisson, maybe irritated by Latude, treats him often enough as a rascal, a colossal mountebank, though Funck-Brentano's study is invaluable by reason of many material facts discovered only after laborious research in manuscripts and documents, in *Mémoires* and *Rêveries* other than those herewith printed, and among shoals of letters written by Latude in his long and voluminous life. These *Mémoires* survive, having their modest position in French literature, after instantaneous success over a century ago: twenty editions were already exhausted in 1793, translations were made into several languages, journals were stuffed with comment and encomiums, and the *Mercure de France* proclaimed that henceforth dutiful parents must teach their children to enshrine such a sublime work.

To-day we may read more objectively, studying these pages as a lurid side-light on French history, but especially as a psychological document, and a record, demonstrably extravagant now and again, always turgescent, of troubles rarely outpaced elsewhere; yet these troubles are not less remarkable than, though glaringly different from, Latude's thrilling experiences subsequent to his liberation after nearly forty years of prison. The dauntless old fellow reached a sort of apotheosis. He, too, like Napoleon, had his star, worshipped it; and he lived to see it at a zenith, glowing, radiant, though a little smudged by its own sulphureous smoke. No man of the time had greater tenacity and skill in promoting adulation, inspiring tenderness, and palming his own high-pitched notions of himself upon others; and he lived to have his eventual good luck well buttered.

He was born on March 23rd, 1725, mothered by one
Jeanneton Aubrespy, an anxious and unhappy spouse-
less woman at Montagnac in Languedoc, whose family
turned from her when she moaned in illegitimate
labour, and forsook her.   She strove to keep alive
and to rear her ill-timed youngling, having had him
baptized Jean Henri; and perchance the worst offence
committed by Latude in his later belligerent career
was his seeming indifference to and neglect of the
patient creature who had spent herself in wretchedness
so that he might thrive.   Evidently the lad had pre-
cocious ability; for, when seventeen, he was graded
as an assistant-surgeon in the Languedoc army.   He
changed his name to Jean Daury at this stage, followed
the wars, served faithfully; and after the peace of
Aix-la-Chapelle, in 1748, he went to Paris with recom-
mendations for surgeons, and excited hopes of worthy
employment: a brisk, adroit young man, handsome
but for traces of smallpox, and already feverously
ambitious, beginning to scheme, eager also to support
his mother at this hour, who remained in Languedoc.

Paris dazzled him, partly demoralized him, suffusing
him with an unstemmed lust for luxury.   He was
generous, care-free, intent to make a name and to
parade like a fearless dandy, sharing sleeping-quarters
in an obscure lodging with his friend Binguet, and
spending most of his leisure and all his money in a
centre of prodigality and gaiety, having superabundant
confidence in himself and no regard for an impoverished
future; boastful, easily roused to fight, equally ready
to play the boon companion.   Consequently, he soon
found himself in a sharp need of cash, and so made his
first recorded effort at swindling, as harsh critics have
it, or perhaps more truly as an instinctive play-actor,
a born comedian engendering his fictions, already fain
to believe in them after the first essay, always forceful
in applying them.   He pretended he had been robbed

and ſtripped to his shirt at the siege of Berg-op-Zoom, the impregnable fortress ſtormed by the French; and now he wrote to the authorities explaining his plight and demanding an indemnity. Indemnities haunted Latude. This tangible cozening failed, as moſt men other than a Latude might have foreknown. He seemed not heavily depressed, having devised another trick, more subtle and perilous, hence more attraćtive and promising to him—Madame de Pompadour being the bait, high game for him. He gives an account of this direfully potent exploit in his *Mémoires*, also the reasons thereof; but some of the faćts are expurgated or transformed, and muſt be sought otherwhere.

Latude had pondered the political intrigues of his age, and doubtless fancied he too might be apt and could soar far in such a miſty atmosphere, he too, like many intelligent and inquisitive Parisians, assuming he knew the hiſtory of the illuſtrious lady, could gauge her charaćter and profit from it. She is prominent in the accounts of what Carlyle named Strumpetocracies; a woman subtle and skilled in her devious passage to fame, endowed with bright sapience of a kind and with enough charm to ensnare a King, and power eventually and indirećtly to rule a Court.

She was born of bourgeois parents at Paris in 1721, suckled by a covetous, affećtionate, intriguing mother, educated by reputable pedants, and married in due season to Normant d'Étioles, nephew to her mother's lover, Tourneham, a gay and cultured *fermier général*; and after contrivings and some mild cheateries and much audacity and courage, she took the magnetic place of the defunćt Madame de Châteauroux, miſtress to Louis XV. The Court was riddled and rotted with irascible faćtions, jealousies, squabbles for position, political treacheries, and so forth; and Madame's enemies were more numerous than her friends, though not so powerful. Her royal lover taxed her brains and her body severely, after the first ecstatic flush; for he appears to have been polygamous by instinct, despotic by temperament, erratic yet ardent, sometimes afraid and, by analogic likelihood, repentant, religious; invariably exacting to a woman who kept her footing and tried to conserve her prestige largely and at last solely by her own necessary astuteness. Madame du Hausset, in her memoirs, speaks of the endless fears of her mistress; who, chillsome in blood, by no means meridional, dreaded that she might cease to be agreeable to her lusty sovereign and would therefore lose his heart; and, by sequence, he might look for her deputy, supplanting her—disastrous possibility for Court favourites. The Duchess de Brancas, Madame's wise good friend, advised her to make herself precious to the King by her gentleness, and needful to him by her intelligence; and thereafter Madame laboured and schemed to be his tacit chief minister, humouring him, controlling him to such an extent that France seems to have been more or less governed from the bedchamber. Madame knew and deplored her own limitations, and understood the King's predilections: her enemies declared that she served as the oblique manageress of his seraglio at the Parc-aux-Cerfs, since she could not demolish it; and, says report, she showed humanity and pity, and gave aid, to the several mothers of his several bastards.

Her steadily increasing power as a factor in the State and a wary director of the impressionable King disquieted some of her friends and thoroughly alarmed her enemies, of whom Maurepas stood as the chief, seconded less overtly by his more cautious fellow D'Argenson. Maurepas, first minister and hitherto beloved of the King, a man of infinite resource, charming and perfidious, says Pierre de Nolhac in his sympathetic account of Madame, had consistently despised the edacious mistresses of his master. He loathed Madame, and sought by means fair and foul to ensure her ruin. She prevailed against him, coaxed and persuaded the King; and Maurepas was sent hence, exiled to Bourges, she having insisted that there were conspiracies to poison her. Madame suffered great tribulation in the midst of her splendour, sure she was menaced without and within, scared day by day, pestered with anonymous and threatening letters, lampoons, satirical verses, and the like, living in constant apprehension of death. She surrounded herself with antidotes to poison, refused to be the first to eat of any dish, even at supper with the King, and had a physician in attendance at the theatre to sample sweetmeats and drinks before she dare take refreshment. Her panics were intensified after the dismissal of Maurepas, who, she supposed, would try to slake vengeance on her either directly or by way of accomplices.

Latude knew the facts, and the fictions, about Madame, hearing gossip widespread from the Court, and he set his nimble wits to work, deciding to pose as her protector, and to be protected in a grateful return, promoted to high office, cognizant that this sort of thing had befallen men less worthy than he in Madame's lavish, often thoughtless, sometimes comic, distribution of her political favours at Court. In April, 1749, he bought six pear-shaped toys made of molten glass, which shattered with a bang when hit smartly on the tapering end. He put four of these innocuous trifles into a cardboard box and fastened the ends to a thread fixed in the lid. Then, having sprinkled the mock-bomb with toilet-powder, alum, and vitriol powder, he enclosed the box in an inner and an outer wrapper, labelled respectively: " Madame, I beg you to open this packet in secret " and : " To Madame the Mar-quise de Pompadour, at Court." He posted the packet. On the evening of the next day he went to Versailles,

where, having succeeded in reaching Madame's head-
valet, and unable to press further, he pitched his tale,
vowing he had overheard two fellows at the Tuileries
as they threatened Madame, and, dogging them, saw
them post something. In his devotion he believed
it was his bounden duty to warn Madame of probable
danger.

Thus he set his stage.

Madame trembled for her life. The King's physician, instructed, opened the box with exceeding great
care, recognized the powdered vitriol, and probably
smiled at a supposed criminal design bungled and
harmless. Madame and the King were shocked, and
investigations began, directed by D'Argenson, who, as
the old friend of Maurepas, no doubt feared for himself
and yearned to exonerate himself by zeal in exposing
a villainy. Latude was arrested on May 1st, after
Saint-Marc, head detective, had compared the script
attached to the fateful packet with an account of the
tale written by Latude on demand. This proved
fatal to the young man. He was sent to the Bastille;
where, interrogated later, and ignorant of the recent
detective work, he persisted in his fable; and yet again
at a second examination. Then he took refuge in
an obstinate silence. These foolhardy tactics added
to the alarm of authority, and Latude was declared to
be a tool in the hands of conspirators. D'Argenson
wrote to Berryer, the lieutenant of police, insisting that
the affair must be of the utmost importance, and no
effort should be spared to discover the truth. When
Latude did in fact confess, he had mystified and teased
his captors to such a pitch that no one believed him.
Year after year he remained in this or that prison, his
first escape from Vincennes having added greatly to
his original offence; and almost until the end he was
considered to be the puppet of dark conspirators, whose
names he would not divulge; for he had failed to

remove the impression derived from his contradictory
fictions immediately after his arrest. His *Mémoires*,
strewn with hyperbole, give an intensely pungent
account of his afflictions, his escapes, his failures,
intrepidity, and cunning; and they break off
abruptly at his capture, wretched sequel to a third
evasion.

He was taken once more to Vincennes, there to
revolve anew in the circle of his miseries, though he
had been within a shred of relative freedom, authority
having decided that they dealt with an imbecile rather
than with a criminal; but escapes from prison were
unpardonable, a third escape hitherto unthinkable to
outraged major and minor policemen. Undoubtedly
Latude, at this time, seared in his nerves and his brain
after perpetuated close confinement, could and did
behave like one deranged. He raved in his cell; and
in further letters to the much scolded and bespattered
Sartine, now lieutenant of police, to whom, as will be
seen from the memoirs, Latude latterly assigned all
his torment, and by whom he meant to be indemnified
prodigiously when at last the triumphant hour should
sound and he might confound his enemies and take his
rightful place in an admiring world; whereas, seemingly,
Sartine had worked, and did work, generously to
persuade his masters to release the poor fellow.

Latude passed from Vincennes to Charenton, the
mad-house, but this change had no effect whatsoever
in reducing the sense of his own power, dignity,
prestige; nor did it impair his curious and fugitive
gift of humour: " Engineer, geographer, and pensioner
of the King at Charenton " he could write of himself,
now past fifty, and after twenty-six years of imprisonment. Two years later, however, his gaolers let him
go, on condition that he should hie himself swiftly to
Languedoc, and stay there; but Paris, the only appropriate setting for such a verbose, histrionic genius,

fascinated and wheedled him. He borrowed money, advertised himself indefatigably, added to his already considerable reputation or notoriety, gained help from princes, began to rise and to unfold his long-mildewed wings; till a smart jerk made end, for the time being, to his soaring. He was peremptorily warned to take himself off to Languedoc at once, or to return to gaol without parleys. He trudged as far as Saint-Bris, forty-three leagues from Paris; and here, according to Funck-Brentano, he sprawled once again in the arms of the police, after attempting to extraƈt cash by threat from a gentlewoman: other hiﬅorians ﬅate that his offence was the writing of his *Mémoires*, which may be the truth of it, for he seems to have had no criminal trial.

Anyhow, to prison he went, after less than a two months' freedom, on this occasion finding himself housed at Bicêtre, a place reserved for low thieves and scoundrels; where again he changed his name, " not wanting to soil his father's title by putting it on the regiﬅer of such an infamous place." His imagination and his diverse talents were now at full tide and he busied himself with projeƈts for helping himself, the King, the Nation, and Humanity at large. He dabbled in sorcery, hobanobbed with spooks; he mesmerized his associates, as he had done in the paﬅ, and would do to the end; he enliﬅed the sympathies and won the aid of the turnkeys, imposing his personality by a sheer force of will when ordinary bribes and simple cajoleries failed. He wrote memoirs of himself and of his sufferings and grievances, and managed to scatter them abroad. A tipsy turnkey loﬅ one of these surcharged missives; and Madame Legros, palpably Latude's good angel, found it in the ﬅreet, read it, and, touched profoundly in her sensibilities, accepted every word of the piteous tale and resolved to save the man or to lose herself in unsparing effort.

Madame Legros, humble by position, living with her spouse on the proceeds from a small haberdasher's shop, had the will of an Amazon and the compassion of a saint; and the most surprising fact in this surprising record is that she succeeded, having influenced Presidents and ministers, the Cardinal de Rohan, advocates, deputies; and she reached the cabinet of the Queen with her story of cruelty and age-long distress. The Marquis de Villette, the friend of Voltaire, impassioned on Latude's behalf, offered a pension of six hundred livres to the prisoner if he would grant the Marquis the honour of securing his liberty. Latude, convinced that his crown in public and private favour loomed brightly on a near horizon, romantic from his heels to his scalp, wrote in reply that since for two years a poor woman had devoted herself to his deliverance, he would be thankless if he transferred his fate to other hands.

Now the French Academy caught the spreading infection, they too beginning to clamour for justice to Latude; and the prison-cell in Bicêtre became a radiating centre of interest and intrigue. Louis XVI refused to be enticed into the movement, gave a flat No to all plaints; notwithstanding, Madame Legros was undismayed; and she had help from the Queen and Madame Necker. In 1783 Breteuil, the Queen's friend, came into power; and a year later, Latude, the Viscount de Latude as he named himself, left prison finally, and with a pension of four hundred livres. Now his hour had verily arrived, and, after another slight hitch, he was allowed to relish his freedom actually in Paris. He lived with the Legros, his benefactors, adoring them, and he basked happily as the subliminal hero of the day, courted, flattered, encircled by Dukes and Duchesses and lesser worshipping fry. Madame Legros also had a pension, she too being a noble figure in Latude's reflected glory;

and his pensions were extended, his miraculous fortunes swollen, by public subscription.

He became the familiar of grand ladies and their attentive daughters, discovering that they were ready almoſt to swound when he told his life-ſtory; and tell it he did without ſtint or hesitatings, here, there, everywhere. "It is difficult for me to know," he writes, "which of these Countesses, Marquises, Duchesses, and Princesses is the moſt human, the moſt tender." He played his grandiloquent part like an Eaſtern potentate, meanwhile suing the inheritors of Madame de Pompadour's eſtates, and others, for damages, obtaining indemnities; nor did this satisfy him, for he had determined that these people, together with Sartine, ought in fairness to pay him at leaſt—one million, eight hundred thousand livres!

Then the Revolution wrought dreadful havoc, and Latude's pensions were reduced, or annulled, though he contrived to keep funds enough for a modeſt comfort. He ceased to call himself a Viscount and displayed himself as one of the venerable fathers of the democratic hour; and he had already published his *Mémoires*, so adding fuel to a flame which otherwise might have dwindled at a time when personalities were about to rise and to fall like jumping-jacks.

Latude neither faltered nor ſtumbled when Napoleon arose to govern the deſtinies of France; and he continued to use his paſt as his particular and produćtive kingdom, claiming the right thereby to speak in all the Courts of Europe, if such should be his need or his imagined duty. He wrote to the Emperor:

> "Sire, I have been five times interred alive and have known misery. It is necessary to have endured great misfortunes in order to have a heart more pitiful than that of moſt men. I have had the immense satisfaćtion during the

Terror of saving the lives of twenty-two unfor-
tunates. . . . If I have braved death to save
life . . . judge, great Emperor, whether my
heart can refrain from interesting itself in you,
the saviour of my beloved country."

Thus, it will be seen, Latude remained true to
himself in old age; nor had he yet reached silence.
In 1804 he sent a copy of his *Mémoires*, and accounts
of his utilitarian projects, to the King of Prussia and
other monarchs, explaining how the sovereigns of
Europe could profit by his, Latude's, genius, suggesting
that, in justice, he should receive a worthy recompense
for allowing rulers to benefit by him. About seven
months later he died at Paris of pneumonia, in his
eighty-first year, no doubt grumbling at the ingratitude
of Kings, and feeling that power to instruct and to
help them yet lay untainted in him, always abundant.

Hazlitt wrote that the three greatest egoists the
world had known, and who had felt their own being
most urgently and exclusively, were Rousseau, Words-
worth, Benvenuto Cellini; and he defied the world
to furnish a fourth. If Hazlitt had examined the
history and the character of Latude, quite likely he
would have supplemented his list, defying the world
to furnish a fifth.

J. M. W.

"DESPOTISM UNMASKED"

OR

MEMOIRS OF HENRI MASERS DE LATUDE

Imprisoned during thirty-five years in various State prisons

" Mortals, respect Rome ; it is no longer in irons."—*Death of Cæsar*, Act i, sc. 1.

4

AUTHOR'S FOREWORD

IN 1787 a pretended history of M. de Latude was published under the title: *History of a Thirty-nine Years' Detention in State Prisons, written by the prisoner himself*. M. de Latude knows the author of this little pamphlet, and he would have much to say to him; but at present he is addressing the public, warning them that he repudiates this History, supposed to have been written by himself, wherein the facts are not always accurate, as is evident from the title alone, which speaks falsely of a thirty-nine years' captivity; otherwise, far from being the *history of his detention*, it is simply that of three facts from his long and unhappy adventures, and has scarcely any resemblance to his true history. M. de Latude accepts and guarantees as true only those of his Memoirs signed by himself with his own hand, as may be seen at the foot of this foreword.

The writer of this book claims, in his turn, to speak of himself for a moment. Ruled by events, he has been forced to produce his work with the utmost speed, and to print it during the writing, having as it were to dictate to three compositors. Thus, inevitably, there will be some inaccuracies or repetitions, for which he craves indulgence. There is fear of being tempted always to use the same colours when the same pictures must be painted frequently.

DE LATUDE.

TO M. DE LA FAYETTE.

MONSIEUR,

It is to the generous defender of liberty that one of the most famous victims of despotism must consecrate his astonishing history to-day.

You were hardly past boyhood when you set off to a new world, there to exercise high virtues, which one day were to honour your country in the eyes of a startled Europe. I was then in irons, forgotten, separated from the world, and the sound of your name penetrated to the depth of my dungeons; an impulsive admiration mingled itself with my frenzy of despair, and immediately I foresaw your future glory.

I regained my freedom, I saw you, I dared to love you. Happy spouse, happy father, adored citizen! posterity will know that you were great: it is for me to show that you were compassionate.

I am, with respect,
Monsieur,
Your very humble and most obedient servant,
DE LATUDE.

MEMOIRS OF HENRI MASERS DE LATUDE

FORMERLY AN ENGINEER

A prisoner in the Bastille and at Vincennes for thirty-five years under the name of DAURY; *at Charenton under the name of* DANGER; *and at Bicêtre under that of* JÉDOR.

*   *   *

YES, for thirty-five years I have vainly belaboured these infernal vaults with my sighs and my despair: my spirit bruised incessantly by fits of rage and distressed by endless pain; all my limbs seared, torn by the weight and friction of my chains; my body gnawed by the most repulsive animals, breathing only putridities in place of air, and, as the acme of horror, succoured and saved whenever death seemed willing to make end to my anguish by snatching me from my tormentors: such was my fate throughout this long sequence of years. All of you for whom time glides and speeds so quickly in the bosom of pleasures and of liberty—and if you can imagine a suspension of its course for the wretched being groaning in the solitude of a dungeon—calculate for a moment how many centuries must have been contained in this frightful period of thirty-five years for him whose torments—ever new, and augmented by those his searching memory extracted from the past—ceaselessly wasted his courage and strength. My purpose is not merely to rouse a cold and sterile pity in you: I make so bold as to instruct you by my misfortunes. When day by day you see so many crimes unpunished,

53

you may learn how a favourite and her unworthy
ministers dared to avenge themselves for a trivial
offence.

*   *   *

I was born on the 23rd of March, 1725, at the
château of Craiseih, near Montagnac in Languedoc,
on an estate belonging to my father, the Marquis de
Latude, knight of the royal and military order of
Saint-Louis, lieutenant-colonel to the regiment of
Orleans Dragoons, who met his death as King's
lieutenant at Sedan.   My education was that of a
gentleman destined to serve his country and his King.
I shall not enter into the details of my early years: the
true history of my life is that of my misfortunes alone.
I showed some ability, and a decided taste for mathematics: this my parents endeavoured to cultivate,
favouring my inclination, which induced me to become
an engineer.   When I was twenty-two, my father
sent me to his friend M. Dumai, chief-engineer at
Berg-op-Zoom, who welcomed me, received me in
the capacity of a supernumerary, and made me wear
the uniform.   I was about to launch myself when,
unfortunately for me, the peace of 1748 was concluded.
My father wished me to take profit from this period
of rest; he sent me to Paris, there to follow my course
in mathematics and to finish my education.   I was
young, I had all the activities of my age, and I experienced perpetually the torments such activities
breed in those who wish to cut a figure, and who take
for talents the agitations of their minds.   I would
have welcomed the good-luck of rising in the world
at no matter what cost.   But I needed patrons to that
end, and I wanted them to be powerful; my vanity, or
rather, my love of glory, sought them in the highest
ranks; for why degrade the passion which, in a young
man, is invariably noble in sentiment and worth a
measure of esteem ?   Anyhow, I was unknown, I

desired to be known; and, seeking means thereto, I consulted my imagination alone: hence the following and consequent notions.

The Marquise de Pompadour reigned supreme at that time. This imperious woman expiated, through a universal hatred, the crime of having led the King to forfeit the love and respect of his people; she had supplemented this crime by sacrificing a beloved minister* to her vengeance, punishing him by disgrace and exile for an ingenious pleasantry. She was named only with mingled disdain and horror, all lips giving utterance to the sentiment that charged all hearts.

On a day in the month of April, 1749, I was at the Tuileries; and two men, seated near me, were giving rein to a most lively indignation against her. The passion apparently inflaming them excited my mind; which, ever directed toward the absorbing aim of all my meditations, gave birth to a project, a supposed certain means, whereby I might win advancement and ensure my fortune. I did not consider that to warn the Marquise de Pompadour of public opinion would be effective; certainly I could have told her nothing she did not already know or suspect. I wanted to signalize my zeal so that, in her gratitude, she would interest herself in my fate. I hastened to Versailles after posting a letter addressed to her enclosing a powder of a quite harmless nature: I told her what I had heard, exaggerating the wish expressed by the two fellows to dispute with others the glory of delivering France from her; I added that I had followed them as far as the general post office, where they carried a packet, which, I assumed, remembering their talk, was suspicious and perhaps contained some very subtle poison.

The first impulse of the Marquise was to express a most spirited appreciation, and to offer a purse full

* Maurepas.

of gold to me; which I refused, telling her I dared aspire to a reward more worthy of her and of myself, and in accord with the facts I gave to her of my position and of my desires. Suspicious and mistrustful, like all tyrants, she wished to have my handwriting; and, under the pretext of recalling and conserving my address, she set me down at her writing-table so that I might do her bidding. The intoxication produced by the success of my plan, and the vivacity of my character, prevented me from detecting a snare; nor did I reflect that in writing two addresses in the same hand I was about to convict myself. I returned home, proud of my work, and already enumerating all the stages of my future grandeur.

The Marquise received the packet: she had tests made on various animals with the powder found therein; and, discovering it to be quite innocuous, and finding by comparison that the two addresses were in a like handwriting, she regarded my thoughtless act as a grossly offensive insult, or rather, as a crime; and she issued the most rigorous orders against me.

On the ensuing 1st of May, and as I indulged in the most sparkling dreams, a detective named Saint-Marc, accompanied by several archers, interrupted my pleasant sleep. At that time I housed at a lodging in the Cul-de-sac du Coq. They flung me into a hackney-coach, and, about eight o'clock in the evening, took me to the Bastille.

I was conducted to a lower hall named the Council Chamber, where I found all the officers of the prison awaiting me. They searched me from head to foot and stripped me of all my clothes: everything I possessed—money, jewels, papers—was taken away; and they dressed me in squalid rags, no doubt already soaked with the tears of innumerable ill-fated men. This ceremony, borrowed from the Inquisition and from highwaymen, passed at the Bastille under the name of "admitting the prisoner." They made me inscribe in a register my entry to the Bastille, then led me to a room in a tower, the Corner Tower. They banged two thick doors on me and left me alone, and without having informed me of my crime or of what my fate would be. The next day, M. Berryer, lieutenant of police at that time, came to interrogate me. I must describe him; for I shall have to speak more than once of this worthy magistrate. How fortunate to be able, when harrowing the compassion of mankind with a story of such great misfortunes, to dwell an instant on the thought of an estimable creature, whose touching sensibility occasionally solaced woe! I shall but rarely enjoy this sad privilege.

M. Berryer inspired confidence by his benignity and kindness. He dared to rise above prejudice in doing good, consulting nothing but his heart and his duty in the exercise of his functions. He is sparsely known to-day, which is not surprising; and in those days he was unknown, save to the miserable. Such a man was out of place at the Court of the Marquise.

I hid from him neither my doings nor my purpose: my candour roused his interest; my action seemed to him merely a youthful frolic, perhaps excusable in view of its object, and assuredly deserving no more than a light punishment. He promised to be my protector in relation to Madame de Pompadour, and to demand my freedom from her; but any man daring to thwart her passion and to avenge her wrongs mildly had scant credit from her. He found her inexorable, and was obliged to avow this to me.

Judge my state of mind at such news!—alone, a prey to my fancies, devoid of hope, without resource, trying unceasingly to discern in the future what my fate would be, and foreseeing only a dreadful abyss! M. Berryer sought to procure every alleviation for me within his power: he gave orders that I should not be deprived of anything, and he sent a companion to me in my wretchedness. This man, Joseph Abuzaglo, a Jew, secret agent in Paris to the King of England, had been betrayed by letters opened in the post, and he was sent to the Bastille. He had some wit; and in any other situation I might have found his society agreeable, and pleasure from intimacy with him; but, instead of relieving each other, we only seemed to extend our mutual miseries and despair. Abuzaglo had a wife and children whom he cherished tenderly, and whose letters were all intercepted cruelly, no news of them coming to him, such being the atrocious system at the Bastille. He bore his captivity with even less courage and fortitude than myself; yet he could entertain hopes, having been especially recommended to M. le Prince de Conti, who had welcomed him warmly; hence he might reasonably flatter himself that efforts would be made to obtain his liberty. He promised to interest the Prince on my behalf; and we swore that the one who first left the prison must, before all else and without stint, concern himself in the deliverance of the other. We were already and eagerly feasting on this idea, beginning to console ourselves; but it did not square with the plans of my persecutors to allow me to enjoy even a hope of changing my fate.

I did not then know that one of the principal duties of the turnkeys was to overhear prisoners as they talked; and doubtless it would have increased their satisfaction so to spy into a prisoner's mind and read his thoughts. I am certain that the promises made to me by Abuzaglo were overheard; and since he had not exaggerated his credit, and because infallibly the first use made of his freedom—soon regained—would have been to try and procure mine, it was resolved to separate and to deceive us.

During September, 1749, about four months after my detention, three turnkeys entered our cell; one of

whom, addressing me, said the order for my release
had just arrived. Abuzaglo fell on my neck, embrace
me tenderly, and begged me to remember our promises.
I believe my first feeling at that moment was joy at
the possibility of breaking his fetters; but alas! this
delicious sensation itself would soon become an added
torment.

Hardly had I crossed the threshold of my prison-
door when I learned that I was being transferred to
Vincennes: my despair at this news may be imagined
from the horror it inspires. Oh, you who read my
words, do not yet exhaust your feelings; for here is
only a prelude to horrors piled without ceasing to make
me suffer! Thus the ever renewed torments over-
whelming prisoners of State were not considered
enough; and game was made by abusing minds which,
seemingly crushed, were coaxed into life again, so to
experience a greater pain. /The usual torturers of
this Inquisition were the turnkeys; the sort of person
fit for such employment, and even inferior as a rule in
conduct to such an office. Their presence was a
misery: they only replied by a painful silence or by
lies to the countless questions addressed to them. / I
have discovered since that Abuzaglo soon obtained
his release: but, believing I had been liberated, hearing,
too, that I in no way concerned myself about him, he
made scant effort to find my whereabouts; and probably
he supposed I merited a forgetfulness similar to that
attributed by him to me.

It will be readily understood that I fell ill in my new
prison. The good M. Berryer came again to comfort
me. He expressed indignation at the treatment imposed on me; but he could neither change the system
of the prisons nor the minds of those charged to
pursue it. He made them give the most comfortable
room in the keep to me, whence I enjoyed a superb
view. What, however, was the use of this privilege ?—

the thought that my removal to this place might promise a long, maybe an endless, captivity would in itself have been enough to poison the most attractive pleasure. My courage was sustained solely by the hope that some day I should procure my freedom; I fancied I could rely on myself alone; and thenceforward I thought of nothing except the means to attain this end.

I noticed an aged churchman who walked each day in a garden forming part of the donjon. I learned that he had been shut up for a considerable time because of his Jansenism. The Abbé de Saint-Sauveur, son of a one-time King's lieutenant at Vincennes, was allowed to come and talk with him in this garden, and often took advantage of the concession. In addition, our Jansenist taught the children of a turnkey to read and to write; thus the Abbé and the children came and went without attracting much attention. The time when these walks occurred nearly squared with my hour for being led out into a neighbouring garden, also within the château enclosure. M. Berryer had ordered that I must be left here for two hours each day, so to take air and to re-establish my health. Two turnkeys came to fetch and to escort me. Occasionally the elder of the pair went straight to the garden, while the other alone opened my prison-doors. For a time I accustomed him to see me descend the staircase more quickly than himself; and, without awaiting him, I joined his associate; hence, when he reached the garden, always he found me with the latter.

One day, when I had resolved to escape at no matter what cost, he had barely opened the door ere I darted to the staircase; and I reached the bottom step before he thought of following me. Here I closed and bolted a door, so to prevent any communication between the two turnkeys while I executed my plan. There were four sentries to trick, the first being at a door invariably shut and leading from the keep. I knocked, the door opened, and I asked briskly for the Abbé de Saint-Sauveur. I said:

"Our priest has been waiting two hours for him in the garden, and I have been running everywhere, but I cannot find him. Lord! he shall pay me for my trouble."

As I spoke I continued to walk on hurriedly. At the end of the archway, under the clock, I found a second sentry, and asked him whether the Abbé de Saint-Sauveur had been gone some time. He said he knew nothing of this; and he let me pass. The same question to the third sentry, on the far side of the drawbridge, brought answer that he had not seen the Abbé.

"I shall soon find him," I shouted, transported with joy.

I ran, I skipped along like a child; and, in this state, I reached the fourth sentry; who, far from suspecting my being a prisoner, was no more surprised than the others to see me running after the Abbé de Saint-Sauveur. I leapt across the threshold of the door and darted out, disappearing from sight. I was free.

Heavens! Whenever I recall this scene my gratitude is as keen as it was then, and once more I enjoy the same intoxication.

Thus, on June 25th, 1750, after about nine months of imprisonment at Vincennes, I had the good fortune to escape.

I hastened over the fields and through vineyards, keeping as far as possible from the high-road; and I managed to hide myself in a lodging at Paris, and could relish the joy of freedom after a fourteen months' captivity.

The first moments were delicious, but did not endure; anxiety soon disturbed this blessed calm: something must be decided. What should I do?

what would become of me? I knew I should be pursued, inevitably; and, if once more I fell into the hands of those from whom I had but now escaped, I should be punished for eluding the tyranny of a woman who never forgave. I was certain of detection if I showed myself; and I ran equal risks if I fled. Furthermore, my condition, my tastes, welded me to the capital: must I, therefore, break all the bonds enchaining me, or must I hide from sight and condemn myself to a captivity more cruel than the one from which I had escaped?

I have related how, hitherto, I had taken counsel only with my head: now, however, mistrusting it, I consulted my heart, but found no better guidance. Until this moment an excessive vivacity had led me into nothing but silliness; and this time an excessive frankness ruined me, and hurled me back into the abyss. I thought fit to judge the Marquise de Pompadour as if she were myself; I believed I might invoke her noble feelings by showing some trust in her, or at least by not appearing to fear her or to doubt her good nature: I anticipated forgiveness, since I felt that, in her place, I should have accorded forgiveness. I did not then know that sentiments and passions differ as widely as those who experience them and correspond with the movements of a virtuous mind or the agitations of a corrupt mind.

I drew up a Memorial, addressed to the King, wherein I spoke of Madame de Pompadour with respect, repenting my fault against her: I entreated that she might be satisfied with the punishment I had suffered; otherwise, if they assumed that fourteen months' imprisonment had not sufficiently atoned for my wrongdoing, then I dared to implore the clemency of the woman I had offended and the mercy of the King. I ended this Memorial with information about the retreat I had chosen, displaying an artlessness that plainly revealed the ingenuousness of my character; which, in itself, ought to have sufficed to ensure pardon for my crime, if I were in effect culpable.

At the château of Vincennes I had become acquainted with Doctor Quesnai, physician to the King and to the Marquise: he had taken some interest in me at that time, offering his services. I set off to find him, and I entrusted my Memorial to him, which he promised to deliver. He kept his word only too well. I have no doubt that the King was touched by my trust in his goodness, but he very rarely followed the promptings of his heart; and how could I expect he would consult his heart alone in a matter concerning the woman on whom he lavished all his thought and affection ? I ought, indeed, to have considered that, irritated by my not addressing myself to her directly, or because of my exposing her injustice and her inhumanity toward me, she would be shamed before her sovereign, and must seek means to avenge a pride wounded so cruelly. Once again, however, I was young; I little knew the heart of men, much less the heart of tyrants; and I was far from imagining that this woman, whose mind must be exhausted daily by so many diverse feelings, could conserve a hatred active enough to track me down without respite and to punish a light offence by so much torment. I paid dearly for my fatal inexperience.

In the Memorial I had indicated the place of my retreat; and they sent thither to find me, and haled me back to the Bastille. In truth, at first they said they arrested me only in order to inquire about the manner of my escape from the Donjon of Vincennes, since it was highly important to prevent other prisoners from imitating my methods, and to make sure of the fidelity of those who kept guard over this château, in case they had facilitated my escape.

Assuredly they would never have extracted this last

avowal from me; but I owed my deliverance solely to
myself, and I recounted naïvely the fashion of this
achievement.   After such a statement I expected the
fulfilment of a promise given to me wherefore my
freedom would be the price of my veracity; I did not
yet know that false promises were the usual formula
when prisoners were about to be enchained afresh;
thus, no doubt, it was intended to wound the souls
of prisoners more cruelly, and to enjoy the pleasure
of multiplying blows to overwhelm them: such practice,
to which I grew accustomed in the sequel, formed part
of the Bastille régime.   On this occasion, far from
giving me my freedom when I had fulfilled the
accompanying condition, they flung me into a dungeon, and tested me by appalling treatment formerly
unknown to me.   However, we will not anticipate
events.

My previous comforter, M. Berryer, came again
to alleviate my woes.   Outside the prison he begged
justice or clemency on my behalf; inside, he tried to
soothe my grief, which seemed less bitter when he
assured me that he shared it.   His exhortations were
so gentle, his advice so affectionate; and his voice
seemed to open a way to his heart.   Oh, you who fill
this august office, could you but understand with what
ease you might lighten the weight of chains borne so
painfully by unhappy wretches!—one word perhaps
would raise their hopes and dry their tears.   At what
a small cost could you appear as gods to them!   Why,
therefore, are you so often but torturers in their sight?

My protector, unable to alter prescribed command,
left me in the dungeon; but he took care that my food
should be the same as before; and, since a little daylight
penetrated into my vault through a loophole, he gave
instruction for me to be supplied with books, pens,
ink, and paper, whenever I made demand.

I used this remedy, this distraction from misery,

for a considerable time; but, after six months, it ceased
to serve against the despair invading me.   My rebellious mind incessantly evoked the thought of my
persecutress and recalled her image only with horror.
What!   Could there be no end either to my sorrows
or to her vengeance ?   This dreadful uncertainty, the
most intolerable of my torments, disturbed my reason
and tore my heart.   In all my pores I felt the fermenting
of an anger stifled too long; and, in access of rage, my
chief need was to give vent to the more than righteous
indignation inflaming me, and which prompted me to
write bad verses.   I was imprudent enough to inscribe
them on the margin of one of the books loaned to
me :

> With neither wit nor charm,
> Being nor fresh nor fine,
> In France the first of lovers may be caught ;
> A proven fact, since Pompadour can shine.

I never imagined that anyone might find these
lines; and I had disguised my handwriting, so to
prevent discovery in the future.   I did not know that
one of the most urgent and strictly executed orders
in the Bastille was the careful and exacting scrutiny
of all books coming from the hands of a prisoner.
My turnkey, after an examination of the volume
containing the above lines, showed it to the governor.
Doubtless, this man, one Jean Lebel, could have
suppressed all trace of the fact with ease and out of
pity for an unfortunate creature soured by misery and
therefore unable to realize what such an imprudence
might expose him to.   Surely the faintest humane
impulse ought to have suggested this; but how expect
like sentiments from a Bastille governor, from one who,
accessory by his position to all the atrocities committed
in the place, must of necessity be insensible, perchance
ferocious in character ?   And where is the honest,
generous man who would consent to gorge his sight

5

on the dire spectacle of misfortune for a lifetime ?
Jean Lebel, in every respect worthy of his tasks, carried
the book to Madame de Pompadour, anxious to get a
reward from her for such zeal and fidelity; in addition,
doubtless, he was not sorry to be assured that he could
enjoy an extension of my imprisonment: such is the
least calculation common to all his tribe; for, interested
in an increase of prisoners, they are resourceful in
keeping those intrusted to them, using to the utmost
whatsoever facilities they may have to attain this end.

The Marquise de Pompadour's fury at sight of my
impertinence may be pictured, after what has already
been revealed touching her character. What! fettered,
crushed by her hatred and vengeance, yet I could dare
to defy and to insult her! She sent for M. Berryer,
showed my verses to him; and, stammering with rage,
she said:

" Now you know your protégé. Dare to beg mercy
from me again!"

As may be conceived, such an event in no way
diminished the horror of my situation; but, since this
could hardly be augmented, the only result was a
prolongation thereof. I remained for eighteen months
in the dungeon; and not until the end of this period
could M. Berryer take the responsibility of having me
brought thence to a room. Moreover, he offered to
procure what, in this hell, one might call a very grateful
privilege—the benefit of having a servant.

Have I previously stated that the turnkeys never
answer any of the questions put to them, and that
their expression is always gloomy and their speech
frigid ? They are strictly forbidden to utter a single
word, unless desirous of cheating an unhappy prisoner;
and then the ordained words are numbered, each
being a mean one and a lie. During exercise, if a
man is fortunate enough to merit this concession, the
sole sight is the atrabilious face of the same turnkey.

Thus permission to have a man in one's room, to whom one can speak of afflictions and confess sorrow, is a very precious favour. He who should find a comforter, a friend, in a faithful and sympathetic servant, may at least relish one truly agreeable possession; but how hope for such good fortune ? I, on the contrary, discovered that this supposed assuagement was merely an additional torment.

I took advantage of M. Berryer's generous offer. My unhappy father, who, even as I, bewailed my misfortune, and would have sacrificed all things to diminish it, consented joyously to pay the board and the wages of a servant. A man named Cochar, native of Rosni, came to me. This fellow might have been all I hoped to find, for he was good, compassionate; he bemoaned my miseries with me, shared and reduced them. I fancied for a space that my heart, less oppressed, might eventually cheat my imagination, and, thus relieved, I might be relatively happy. However, I did not long harbour illusions potent enough to temper my fate. Poor Cochar endured the weariness of his captivity only for a little time: he groaned, he wept, and at last fell ill. When a servant took office with a prisoner in the Bastille, he shared his master's fate, set free with him, or dying in prison at his side. The unfortunate young man needed only to breathe the fresh air to ensure his recovery; but our plaints, our prayers, failed to obtain his salvation from our assassins. They wanted to glut me with the cruel picture of this wretched man's anguish as he died near me and for me; nor was he taken from my room until he had breathed his last sigh. Has the Inquisition ever accumulated such horrors ? . . .

Oh, you who devote your tears and a well-deserved pity to the fate of this poor man, pause to reflect on mine! I was no more guilty than he; he was a victim of his cupidity, I of injustice and an infamous persecution. Unquestionably, the sentiment inspired by this idea redoubled the agitation and torment of my spirit. Certainly Cochar was not free, nevertheless he lacked nothing, and his mind and his feelings were calm and tranquil. I, on the other hand, borne down by the overpowering weight of hatred, suffered new torture at each breath; my sensibilities were enfeebled, my blood turned rancid in my veins, and every day I felt a distortion, an annihilation, of my whole being. This man, however, could bear only three months in such a plight; whereas I have endured for thirty-five years. What do I say?—plight! Ah! These three months were more serene than any I spent in prison. Then, at least, I was not chained in a dungeon, stretched on filthy rotten straw; then, I was not reduced to fighting for putrid food with animals; then, my body was not pasture for the insects, devouring it since . . . I pause: my mind quails before this picture, though the horror of the ills I suffered is but faintly envisaged!

Uncertainty as to the fate of the unhappy Cochar had crushed me; and I almost surrendered to my wretchedness. M. Berryer, to distract me, used a device employed formerly: he gave me a companion nearly my own age, a young man full of activity, sprightliness and wit, one guilty of a crime similar to mine, victim to a like persecution. He had written a letter to the Marquise de Pompadour, informing her of public opinion, outlining the course she must pursue to overcome it and to retain the confidence of her King; and since the nation was, in fact, attached to her chariot, he urged her to make herself worthy of esteem, and indicated the means.

This young man, D'Alègre, a native of Carpentras, had lamented for three years in the Bastille his disastrous proffer of advice, the haughty prostitute having vowed a hatred as implacable against him as against me; and she made him suffer in the same fashion.

D'Alègre likewise aroused the kindly interest of the compassionate Berryer; and he and I displayed a similar impatience, harassing Berryer with letters and petitions, which never wearied him. He kept us informed of his efforts, the steps he took, and sometimes of his hopes; and at last, one day, he came to announce the woeful news that our persecutress, sick of our complaints and of his, had sworn that her vengeance should be eternal and so forbade any further mention of us; nor did he conceal from us that only the fall or the death of such a fury could make end to our oppression.

My companion broke down under his grief; mine, however, produced a very different effect, giving me the courage and the energy of despair. In such circumstances, only two ways lay open to men yet youthful: to die, or to escape. To any man having the least idea of the Bastille and its position—of the enclosure, the towers, and the system, also the incredible precautions multiplied by despotism so to enchain its victims more surely—the project and the sole thought of escape must appear as the outcome of delirium and, seemingly, can inspire nothing but pity for poor wretches so destitute of sense as to risk such an attempt. Nevertheless I was thoroughly sane when I formed this resolve; and, as will be seen, a most uncommon mind and perhaps a very level head were necessary to devise, ponder, and to execute such a plan.

Here I pause, recalling to my readers the vow I have made to say no word incompatible with the most rigid truth. Whether they will believe themselves transported to some new sphere, in reading my subsequent narrative, or whether they may credit me with magical power, I leave to the free play of imagination; so far as I am concerned, I shall recount facts alone.

It was useless to think for an instant of escaping from the Bastille through the doors, since every physical impossibility combined to render that way impracticable: the last resort, therefore, led through the air. Certainly we had a chimney in our room, the shaft of which emerged at the top of the tower; but, like all Bastille chimneys, this was encumbered with gratings and bars, in several places barely allowing free passage even to the smoke. If we could reach the summit of the tower we should have an abyss of about two hundred feet beneath us; and, at the base, a moat dominated by an excessively high wall, which had to be scaled. We were alone, without tools, without materials, and spied on at each moment of the day and night; watched over meanwhile by a multitude of sentries who surrounded the Bastille, apparently investing it.

So many obstacles, so many dangers, did not discourage me. I sought to impart my idea to my comrade: who sank into a torpor, thinking I must be mad. Thus I was obliged to busy myself alone with this scheme, to think it out, foreseeing the host of frightful difficulties opposed to the execution, finding means to overcome all. To succeed, we must climb to the apex of the chimney, and in spite of the numerous and hampering iron gratings. A ladder of at least two hundred feet would be required for the descent from the top of the tower into the moat; and a second, necessarily of wood, to climb thence. In the event of my procuring materials, I must be able to hide them from espionage, and to work noiselessly, deceiving the crowd of attendants, cozening their senses, and for several months thus to trick their sight and hearing. How could I tell! It was essential to foreknow and to allow for a mass of obstacles continuously renewed, which, each day, and every instant of the day, would crop up, one created by the other, arresting and thwarting the application of my plan, maybe one of the boldest ever conceived by the imagination or carried through to an end by human industry. Reader, this

I achieved! and, once again, I swear I am telling only
the exact truth. Now let us follow all my operations
in detail.

The first consideration was to discover a place where
we could hide our tools and materials from sight, in
the event of our being clever enough to get such
things. By dint of hard thinking I grasped what
seemed to me a most happy idea. I had inhabited
several different rooms in the Bastille; and invariably
when those above and below were occupied I could
hear clearly any noise made in the one or the other.
On this occasion I heard the movements of the prisoner
above, and nothing whatsoever from below; I felt sure,
however, that someone must be there. By calculation
I hit on the notion of a possible double floor, divided
by a little space. The following are the means I
employed to convince myself.

In the Bastille there was a chapel where one mass
was said each day, and three were said of a Sunday.
This chapel had four small cabinets disposed so that
the priest could never see any of the prisoners, who in
turn, and by means of a curtain drawn aside only for
the elevation, could never look directly at the priest.
Permission to attend mass was a special favour granted
only after much difficulty. This M. Berryer obtained
for us, likewise for the prisoner who occupied room
No. 3, the one beneath ours.

I determined to take a rapid survey of this room
when, on coming from mass, I could steal a moment
before the prisoner would be shut in again. I suggested to D'Alègre a means of helping me to this end:
I instructed him to put his pocket-case in his handkerchief and, when we reached the second floor, to withdraw his handkerchief in such fashion that the case
would fall to the bottom of the stairs; then he must
ask the turnkey to go and pick it up. This man,
Daragon, is yet alive. Our little manœuvre was

wholly successful. Whilst Daragon ran after the case
I ascended quickly to room No. 3. I drew the bolt
of the door, examined the ceiling, and noted that it was
not more than ten and a half feet high; I closed the
door again, and counted thirty-two steps from this
room to our own; I measured the height of each step,
and, as a result of calculation, found that there was
a space of five and a half feet between the floor of our
room and the ceiling of the one below. This could
be filled neither with stones nor wood; for such weight
would have been tremendous. Accordingly, I concluded that there must be a sort of drum, an empty
space, of four feet between floor and ceiling.

We were shut in, the bolts were shot; and I fell on
D'Alègre's neck and embraced him rapturously, drunk
with hope and assurance. I said:

" My friend, patience, courage; we are saved!"

I told him of my observations and calculations, and
continued:

" We can hide our ropes and materials—all I need.
We are saved."

" What!" he said; " then you have not ceased to
dream? Ropes, materials! Where are they? Where
can we get them?"

I pointed to my trunk, saying:

" Ropes!—as many as we need. This trunk holds
more than a thousand feet."

I spoke ardently; and, full of my idea, of the ecstasy
provoked by my new hopes, I seemed inspired to him.
He fixed his glance on me, and, in tones of the most
touching and the most tender concern, he said:

" My friend, return to your senses and try to calm
this frenzy possessing you. Your trunk, you say,
holds more than a thousand feet of rope. I know as
well as you what it contains: there is not one single
inch of rope."

" What! Have I not a large quantity of linen,

thirteen dozen and a half shirts, a great many towels, stockings, caps, and other things?* Will they not furnish us with ropes? We can unravel them—thus our ropes!"

D'Alègre, thunderstruck, understood at once the full extent of my plan and notions: hope and the love of liberty never die in the heart of man, and were merely numbed in his heart. Almost immediately I warmed him, I fired him, with my ardour. However, he could not keep pace with me: and I had to meet a huddle of objections, and to rid him of all his fears. He said:

"How are we going to wrench all the iron gratings from our chimney? Where shall we get the materials for the necessary wooden ladder, and find tools for all this work? We do not possess the happy art of creating."

I answered:

"My friend, genius creates, and we have the genius of despair to direct our hands. I repeat: we shall be saved."

* Many people at this point may exclaim at exaggeration, and will not believe that anyone could have so prodigious a quantity of linen; they will conclude that I have only assigned it to myself here as a necessary means to the denouement of my fable. This was the way the English reasoned in the main when, some years ago, a brief account of the escape was translated into their language. My respected and virtuous friend M. le Chevalier de Pongens, then in London, reported to me the impossibility of convincing those with whom he spoke of the matter; they denied the likelihood of this fact, and therefore assumed that all other facts must be fabulous. The explanation is simple; for the best-furnished wardrobes in England contain scant linen, and it is much the same in Paris; but I may say, to meet objections, that the opposite extreme is usual in the provinces. There the custom is to accumulate a considerable, sometimes an astonishing, supply. Thus, if one remembers that I had been brought up in the provinces, and that my parents, in sending me away, expected me to be long absent, it will easily be imagined that my statement may be true; moreover, I bought many things very cheap at the pillage of the town of Berg-op-Zoom.

We had a folding table, supported by two iron hinge-pins: these we sharpened by whetting them on a floor-tile; and in less than two hours, and with our tinder-box steel, we fabricated a good penknife, which served to make two handles to these hinge-pins, whose chief use would be to dig the iron gratings from our chimney.

In the evening, after all the daily inspections were over, we raised one of the floor-tiles with the aid of our picks, and set ourselves to delve in such sort that in less than six hours we had pierced the floor: then we saw that my conjectures were well founded, discovering a space of four feet between the floor and the ceiling beneath. We replaced the tile, which showed no signs of removal.

These preliminaries completed, we unstitched two shirts and their hems, and drew the threads out one by one; we knotted them together and so made a certain number of bundles, which, subsequently, we fashioned into two large balls, each having fifty threads sixty feet long: we plaited them together and so obtained a rope about fifty-five feet long, wherewith we made a twenty-foot ladder, destined to hold us suspended above while we removed the bars and the iron points arming our chimney. This task proved the most painful and the most troublesome, demanding six months' toil; and the mere thought of it makes one shudder. We could work only by doubling our bodies, racking them in exceedingly awkward postures; nor could we endure this position for more than an hour, nor descend without bleeding hands. The iron bars were bedded in a very hard mortar, which could be softened only by blowing water from our mouths into the holes we made.

The laboriousness of our task may be imagined when I say that we were content if, in an entire night, we removed but a fraction of the mortar. As fast as we tore out a bar of iron, we had to replace it in its hole, so to avoid detection during the frequent inspections imposed on us; and in such fashion that we could remove the bars when the moment to escape arrived.

After six months of this cruel and stubborn work we occupied ourselves with the wooden ladder needed to mount from the moat to the parapet, thence to the governor's garden. This ladder must be twenty-five feet long. To such an end we used the wood supplied to warm us—logs from eighteen to twenty inches long. We could not do without pulley-blocks, and many other things for which, indispensably, we must furnish ourselves with a saw: and I made one with an iron candlestick, by means of the second half of the steel, the other having been transformed into a penknife, or small blade. With this piece of steel, the saw, and the pins, we reduced the size of our logs, morticed and tenoned them, and fitted one into the other, each mortice and tenon having two holes in which to fix a rung, and two bolts to prevent it from slipping. We made only one side for our ladder, and twenty rungs, each fifteen inches long; and, the upright being three inches in diameter, each rung jutted out six inches on either side. At every section of the ladder we bound the rung to its bolt with twine, consequently, we could easily mount at night. We hid each completed and perfected section under the floor as fast as we made it.

With the same tools we fitted our workshop, making compasses for ourselves, a square, ruler, winder, pulleyblocks, rungs, and so on, all things—as may be imagined—being always carefully hidden in our storehouse. One danger, already foreseen, could be avoided solely by rigorous precaution. I have previously mentioned that, apart from the frequent inspections made by the turnkeys and various officers of the Bastille, one of the customs of the place was to spy on the actions and to overhear the talk of prisoners, and at moments the least expected. We could shelter ourselves from view by doing our principal work only at night, and taking the utmost caution to hide the slightest trace; for a wood-shaving, any scrap of rubbish, might betray us; but, in addition, we had to cheat the ears of our spies. We talked without end of our project, and by necessity; and somehow we had to avoid, anyhow to avert, suspicion by confusing the notions of whoever might overhear us. Therefore we contrived a special dictionary for ourselves, assigning a name to each of the things we used. We called the saw *fawn*, the winder *Anubis*; the picks *Tubalcain*, from the name of the first man who discovered the art of using iron; the hole made in the floor to hide our materials in the drum became *Polyphemus*, an allusion to the lair of the famous Cyclops; the wooden ladder, *Jacob*, recalled the idea of the one named in Scripture; the rungs were *shoots*; our ropes, *doves*, because of their whiteness; a ball of thread was *our little brother*; the penknife, *bow-wow*, and so forth. If anyone came into the room and either of us saw something lying in sight, he uttered the word *fawn*, *Anubis*, *Jacob*, etc., while the other flung his handkerchief or a towel over the object, and so hid it.

We were ceaselessly on the watch, and were lucky enough to elude detection on the part of all our spies.

The first operations mentioned above being complete, we began on the big ladder: this had to be at least 180 feet long. We set ourselves to unravel all our linen; shirts, towels, caps, stockings, drawers, handkerchiefs—everything that could furnish us with thread or silk. Immediately we had made a ball, we hid it in *Polyphemus*; and, when we had a sufficient quantity, we spent an entire night in twisting the rope. I defy the most clever rope-maker to fabricate one with more art.

The Bastille was surrounded on the upper part by

an edge that jutted out three or four feet, which, naturally, would cause our ladder to swing and to twist as we went down—more than enough to confuse and flurry the steadiest head. To obviate this inconvenience, and to prevent ourselves from falling and being mangled in the descent, we made a second rope, about 360 feet long. This could be run through a pulley-block, a kind of wheelless pulley, so to speak, thus to prevent the rope's getting caught between the wheel and sides of the pulley, so that whoever descended might not find himself hung in the air without means of continuing. Then we made sundry shorter ropes, with which to attach our ladder to a cannon, or to supply unforeseen needs.

When all these ropes were finished, we measured them, having 1,400 feet: subsequently we made 208 rungs, alike for the rope and the wooden ladder. Another inconvenience to be avoided was the noise the rubbing of the rungs against the wall might make as we were descending. We made a sheath for each rung out of the linings of our dressing-gowns, vests, and waistcoats.

We spent eighteen entire months continuously at work on these preparations, nor was this all: we had made thorough provision for reaching the summit of the tower and for our descent to the moat, there being two methods for issuing thence: one, to climb on to the parapet, and from it to the governor's garden before descent into the moat near the Saint-Antoine gate; but this parapet, necessary to cross, was invariably lined with sentries. We could chose a very dark and rainy night when the sentries would not parade to and fro, hence we could manage to escape them; yet there might be rain while we climbed our chimney, and calm, serene weather at the moment of our arrival on the parapet; we might meet the rounds-major, who inspected it continually, in which event we could not possibly hide ourselves, since lights were always carried, and so we should be lost for ever.

The other expedient increased our difficulties, but was less dangerous and consisted in making our way through the wall that separated the Bastille moat from the moat of the Saint-Antoine gate. I realized that in the numerous floodings of the Seine—which, occurring, filled this moat—the water would probably dissolve the salt contained in the mortar, making it less difficult to break; therefore, and by this means, we might succeed in piercing through the wall. However, we needed a drill with which to make holes in the mortar for securing the points of the two iron bars, to be taken from our chimney, and with these two bars we could remove the stones and make a passage. We elected to try this expedient. Consequently, we made a drill with the pin from one of our beds, attaching a handle in the form of a cross.

The reader who has followed in detail these interesting occupations doubtless shares all our feelings of agitation; oppressed, like us, with hope and fear, he hastens the moment when finally we can attempt our flight. This was fixed for Wednesday, February 25th, 1756, the eve of Shrove Tuesday, when, the river being in flood, there were four feet of water in the Bastille moat, and in that of the Saint-Antoine gate, whither we sought deliverance. I filled my leathern portmanteau with a complete suit of clothes for each of us, so that we could make a change, if we were lucky enough to effect our escape.

Directly after dinner had been served, we put our major rope-ladder together, that is, we inserted the rungs; we hid this under our beds, and from sight of the turnkey, when he should come on his prescribed rounds during the day; then we arranged our wooden ladder in three pieces, slipped the iron bars necessary for piercing the walls into their sheath, to prevent

them from making any sound; and we provisioned
ourselves with a bottle of scubac with which to warm
and to invigorate ourselves after labouring in water
up to our necks for more than nine hours. These
arrangements having been made, we awaited the
moment when our supper would be brought to us;
and at laſt the time came.

I climbed the chimney firſt, and, though I suffered
from rheumatism in my left arm, I paid sparse attention
to the pain, having soon to endure something much
sharper; for I had taken none of the precautions
cuſtomary among chimney-sweeps, and soot-duſt
almoſt choked me. These fellows proteƈt their elbows
and knees with leathern guards—and I had nothing
of the sort; therefore I was skinned to the quick in all
my limbs, and blood ſtreamed down my hands and
legs. In this ſtate I reached the top of the chimney;
where, at once, I let down a ball of twine, having thus
furnished myself. To this D'Alègre attached the
end of the cord faſtened to my portmanteau; which
I drew up, untied, and flung on to the platform of the
Baſtille; and we raised the wooden ladder, the two iron
bars, and the other packages, in a similar manner,
ending with the rope-ladder, one end of which I let
down, so to help D'Alègre in his ascent, meanwhile
securing the reſt by means of a thick bolt made for
the express purpose: this I passed through the rope,
laying it crosswise on the chimney shaft—consequently
my companion avoided covering himself with blood
as I had done. Now I descended from the chimney-
top, where I had been in a moſt uncomfortable position;
and we found ourselves on the Baſtille platform.

Here we arranged all our effeƈts promptly: we began
by coiling our rope-ladder, making a heap four feet in
diameter and one foot thick. We rolled it on to the
tower named the Treasure Tower, which, to us, seemed
moſt suitable for our descent; and we fixed one end to

a piece of cannon, let the ladder run gently down the
length of the tower, attached our pulley-block with
the 360-foot rope: I tied this pulley-rope around my
body, and D'Alègre played it out by degrees as down
I went; yet, in spite of this provision, I swung out
into air at each motion. My position may be figured
in accord with the shudders provoked by the mere
thought of such a thing. Finally, and without mishap,
I arrived at the moat. Immediately D'Alègre lowered
my portmanteau and the rest of the stuff; and happily
I found a slight eminence rising above the water—
which now filled the moat—and on this I placed them.
My companion then followed me in the same fashion,
but with a greater ease; for, by holding the end of the
ladder as firmly as I could, I prevented an excessive
vacillation. When the pair of us had landed, we
could not avoid a slight regret at the impossibility of
taking our rope and the materials we had used* with
us—these precious and rare memorials of human
industry, and perhaps of virtues inspired by a love of
freedom.

The rain had ceased. We heard the sentry as he

* On the 16th of July last, after the taking of the Bastille, I presented myself and found, with inexpressible delight, my rope-ladder,
the wooden ladder of which I have spoken, and most of the other
things ; they were shut down under a kind of cage and had been kept
as if they were precious, and made to provoke a certain amazement
and admiration : also, there was an official report, signed February 27th,
1756, by one Chevalier, major of the Bastille, and by the commissary
Rochebrune, which verifies all the facts I have described. In addition,
I found letters from the ministers, and other documents concerning
myself, which I shall have to deal with in the course of these Memoirs.

All these things were carried to the Assembly of the Commune,
who gave orders for the whole to be returned to me, and as a possession
due to me by every right. They were exhibited subsequently at the
last *salon*, where they attracted a general attention ; and at the present
time the rope-ladder is in the hands of a person who proposes to show
it in the principal towns of France, and in England, as one of the most
glorious trophies ever ascribed to liberty.

walked at no more than a stone's throw from us; accordingly we were obliged to forgo our design of mounting on to the parapet, and of escaping by the governor's garden. We decided to use our iron bars and to attempt the second method, explained above. We went straight to the wall separating the Bastille moat from that of the Saint-Antoine gate; and, without respite, we began our toil. At this precise spot there was a small ditch six feet wide and a foot and a half deep, and this increased the height of the water. Elsewhere the water would not have reached above our middles, whereas here it came to our armpits. A thaw had set in only a few days ago, hence the water was yet strewn with pieces of ice; and here we remained for nine solid hours, our bodies exhausted by a task of exceeding great difficulty, our limbs numbed with the cold.

Scarcely had we begun when I saw a rounds-major approaching, twelve feet above our heads; and his lantern lighted our lair clearly. Our only resource, to prevent discovery, was to duck under water; and we were obliged to repeat this manœuvre at each visit, thus several times during the night. May I be forgiven for narrating another event of the same kind, which, in the first instant, gave me a mortal fright, but ended by seeming ludicrous to me? I recount it in a strict observance of the promise not to leave any detail untold, for my object is not to enliven this tale or to raise a smile.

A sentry, walking on the parapet, a very short distance from us, reached our particular spot and drew up immediately above my head. I thought we were discovered, and I had a frightful shock; but, instantly, I heard that he had paused only to make water, or, rather, I felt this, for not one drop escaped my head and face; and I was forced to throw away my cap and to rinse my hair as soon as he had passed on.

6

At last, after nine hours of work and of apprehension, and after having pulled out the stones one by one with an unimaginable toil, we succeeded in making a hole wide enough to pass through and in a wall four and a half feet thick: and we dragged ourselves through. Already our spirits were beginning to rejoice; but we encountered a danger hitherto unforeseen, and before which we nearly succumbed. We were crossing the Saint-Antoine moat to reach the Bercy road, and had hardly gone twenty-five paces when we fell into an aqueduct in the middle, and with ten feet of water over our heads, and two feet of slime preventing us from movement or a step to reach the further edge of the aqueduct, one no more than six feet wide. D'Alègre threw himself on me, all but knocking me down: we were lost; for, without strength enough left to pick ourselves up again, we should perish in this bed of filth. I felt myself seized, and I hit out violently and forced D'Alègre to release me; and, with a corresponding motion, I sprang, and managed to get out of the aqueduct. I plunged my arm into the water, seized D'Alègre by the hair, and drew him to my side. Quickly we were outside the moat; and we found ourselves on the high-road just as five o'clock sounded.

We fell into one another's arms, transported by a like feeling, clasping each other fast; and we prostrated ourselves to express our intense gratitude to God for snatching us from so many perils. Such impulses may be imagined, but they cannot be described.

This first duty fulfilled, we thought of changing our clothes; and then it was that we realized the excellence of our precaution whereby we had provided ourselves with a portmanteau full of dry things: our limbs were numbed with the wet, and, as I had expected, we felt the cold far more now than during the nine consecutive hours passed in water and ice; we were alike incapable of undressing and of dressing ourselves, and were obliged mutually to assist each other. Finally we hired a hackney-coach and were taken to the house of M. de Silhouette, Chancellor to the Duke of Orleans, whom I knew well, feeling sure he would receive us with favour; unfortunately, however, he was at Versailles, so we took refuge with an honest man, equally well known to me, at the Abbey of Saint-Germain; one named Rouit, a native of Digue in Languedoc, and a tailor.

The loss of two victims at one stroke would be too much for the Marquise de Pompadour; and, since she seemed so greatly desirous of tormenting us, she was certain to give way to considerable rage when she learned that, by our flight, we deprived her of her precious enjoyment. Furthermore, she would fear the effects of our too just resentment: we might unmask all the horrors she had inflicted on us to the public, horrors to which so many wretched men were yet subjected; we might take all fellow-citizens into our confidence touching this matter of our pains, and the whole of France would share our indignation. This she knew; and we are assured that she never released any of those whom she flung into chains; she immured their frenzies and their sighs for ever within the circle of dungeon walls.

We were well informed as to her fears and the measures she took, as a rule, to calm them, and we had no doubt that great efforts would be made to discover us. On this occasion I was not tempted to go and lay myself at her feet, nor did I hesitate to banish myself; but it would have been highly imprudent to show ourselves at this pass: accordingly we remained hidden for nearly a month with the honest man who sheltered us. We decided not to set off together; for, if one were discovered, the other might profit by this ill-luck.

D'Alègre went first, disguised as a peasant, proceed-

On the evening of the next day I reached Brussels. In 1747 I had spent part of the winter in the town, so I knew it already. I descended at the Coffi, in the Town-hall square, where D'Alègre had appointed to meet me. I inquired for him of the innkeeper, who told me he did not know what had become of him. I asked the fellow several further questions. I pressed him; he hesitated, and his constrained manner told me all. I understood what had happened to my ill-fated companion, and what no doubt awaited me. I affected a serene air, and left his house, to hide my pain and fear elsewhere. I had announced that I should want a room, and would return for supper at about ten o'clock; and I feigned business and left the town forthwith.

D'Alègre would certainly have awaited me at the inn; and he knew almost exactly the moment of my arrival, and could not have failed at least to leave a note informing me of the reason and the length of his absence, had he been obliged to go out: his utter silence, the host's embarrassment and equivocal remarks when I asked for news, instructed me only too clearly that D'Alègre had been discovered, and that, therefore, no doubt, and shortly, I too should be discovered. Consequently I did not hesitate to pursue my way, and, without loss of time, to book a place on the Antwerp boat, which left at nine o'clock precisely. I entered a neighbouring tavern, where I found a young Savoyard with whom I might travel. His wife and some relations were with him, and they remained in his company until his departure. This Savoyard, a chimney-sweep by trade, hearing that I would embark with him, came and talked to me. As I have said, I wore servant's clothes: his were tolerably clean, and he thought we could journey together amicably. We were soon on extremely good terms. He was making his way to Amsterdam, and thither I had resolved to go in search of a sure retreat. He spoke Dutch quite well, and offered to serve as guide and interpreter. We sat down at table together, and our companionship enchanted him; but I was far from the joyous calm he seemed to relish. We set off. As we continued, I asked him whether anything new had happened in Brussels, where, I said, I had lacked the time to stay. Conceive my astonishment when I heard him recount as an interesting fact the sad adventure of which I might become one of the heroes! Although I ought to have been prepared, in a fashion, for this shock, I shuddered with dread and felt my blood run cold. He told me that, of the two prisoners who had escaped from the Bastille at Paris, one, reaching Brussels recently, had descended at the Coffi, where, after having at first appeared in a peasant's dress, suddenly he had been noticed in a different costume as he walked about and ate with well-known military men and other notables. An officer of justice named Laman had received an order to arrest the prisoner and had conducted him to his house, where, under pretext of taking his name and qualifications, he had shut him in until the next morning, when he handed him over to the provost-marshal of Brussels, who sent him as far as the gates of Lille, under a safe and sound escort; and here he was delivered into the hands of a French police-officer, who had followed the troop from Brussels. My Savoyard added that he had learned these details from Laman's servant, a friend of his, who had begged him to keep the secret, since it was important not to spread the fact abroad, otherwise the escape of the second prisoner might be facilitated, for whom they were likewise on the watch, and who would certainly be unable to avoid the many arrangements made for his arrest.

What were my new feelings now! And in face of this man—who at all costs must suspect nothing—how could I present a serene and tranquil appearance, with a heart lacerated so cruelly and a mind so distraught! I was alternately overcome with pity for poor D'Alègre and fear for myself, and dumbfounded by the host of reflections absorbing me; yet I must seem calm. I made up my mind without hesitation. From the moment I was expected and watched for, undoubtedly my movements would be divined and my tracks followed: infallibly the innkeeper of the Coffi must have recognized me, and that in itself was enough to make me dread arrest at any instant. Our pitiless enemy had managed skilfully to get the unfortunate D'Alègre arrested in a foreign country, and there was nothing she would not undertake to slake her rage; thus, obviously, I ran the same risk as he; therefore I must change my route and foil the designs of those who sought me; for, naturally, they would believe I was flying toward Amsterdam. Moreover, it behoved me to divert the suspicions of my Savoyard, unless I had been lucky enough to avoid rousing them. I asked if the Rotterdam boat passed Berg-op-Zoom. He said No. I knew this fact more surely than he, but I feigned astonishment, saying I had to obtain money on a bill of exchange in that town. I expressed regret at being unable to finish my journey with him, and we pledged ourselves to meet again at Amsterdam. We reached Antwerp, where the boat stops, and I left him; and, to console him in his loss of me, I gave him sundry provision of bread, ham, and brandy, which I possessed. My generosity delighted him; and he wished to put me in the way of getting to Berg-op-Zoom, while awaiting the hour of embarkation, so to show his gratitude to me.

Scarcely had I lost sight of him when I changed my direction, nor did I pause until I reached Dutch soil. I was utterly convinced that on the arrival of the Amsterdam packet I should have found some officer of the Brussels mounted police waiting for me, who, by this or that means, would succeed in arresting me. Poor D'Alègre's ill-luck proved that nothing was sacred to the Marquise de Pompadour.

I had seven louis when I left Paris; and only one remained on my arrival at Berg-op-Zoom. I lodged in a garret at eight sous a night; and my first care was to write to my father. I had been mightily surprised to find no letters from him at Brussels, as I had expected: I have since learned that these were intercepted by the French police-officer appointed to spy for me there. I described my plight to my father, knowing his feelings, never doubting his readiness to send help to me: I told him I meant to go to Amsterdam, and besought him to address his letters thither. With the trifle of cash remaining to me I must pay my fare on the packet from Berg-op-Zoom to Amsterdam; and then I should have three livres and ten sous. Much time must elapse ere I could hear from my father. There were only two ways open to me: either I must beg, or feed myself on herbs; the first revolted me, so I did not hesitate to choose the second. In my determination, I had trusted to my courage rather than to my physical prowess; for necessity reduced me to the level of the animals, though nature had refused me the organs of an animal: my stomach rejected such sorry aliments watered solely by my tears. I hoped I might temper the crudity of these herbs, and so reduce the subsequent pains, if I ate them with a coarse rye-bread, locally named *Rockenbrod*, stuff as black and heavy as a clod, of which I bought four pounds, sole supply for the journey. Such was my state when I set out for Amsterdam.

As may be imagined, I made few advances toward other travellers on the packet; for a display of my misery would humiliate me, and I feared their pity. Thus in complete prostration, and, so to speak, in the surrender of all our sentiments, self-esteem yet remains, alone surviving the rest! Nevertheless I could not prevent myself from looking occasionally at one of my companions, whose severe expression and harsh appearance drew attention and provoked apprehension. He was called Jean Teerhoost, a native of Amsterdam, where he conducted a sort of tavern in a cellar. He scrutinized me closely and seemed chiefly to take note of my frugal diet; he accosted me, thinking he had discovered me, and, in a tone humiliating at first, and finally inspiring confidence—since it was the voice of truth—he said in bad French:

"Good God! By the way you eat you seem to have more hunger than cash."

I confessed awkwardly that he was not mistaken; and he said no more until the hour of food, when he led me to a table on which he had spread his supplies. He said:

"No compliments, Master Frenchman! You just sit down and eat and drink with me."

We commenced to talk from that moment; and soon after I perceived that, under a coarse exterior, this man united the most pleasing qualities, doing good without ostentation, by impulse, almost by instinct, while seeming ignorant of and unconcerned with such things. Sometimes he appeared to understand the delicate art of sparing the susceptibilities of wretched folk needing succour: but, palpably, this too arose in him naturally; he begged a slight assistance from me, so to distract my thoughts from the genuine service he rendered to me. When I told him I came from Languedoc, he said he knew a man from that part of the country, one who, no doubt, would be pleased to help me. Immediately we reached Amsterdam, he directed me to the house of this fellow-countryman, Martin by name, who proved to be a Picardian, and the most unfeeling, repulsive creature I ever met.

His greeting disclosed the chagrin inspired in him by the mere notion of doing a kind deed; and almoſt at once I reassured him by taking my leave.

Jean Teerhooſt, convinced that I should receive the moſt abundant aid from M. Martin, was waiting to congratulate me; and my depression and tears exposed my diſtress to him; for, at this moment, I abandoned myself to all the oppressive thoughts engendered by my situation. Compelled to fly from my country, alone in a foreign land, over three hundred leagues from my kinsmen, without help, resources, friends, or protectors!—what would become of me? My generous Dutchman read my mind unerringly. He came to me, took my hands, and said:

"Do not weep. I won't forsake you. I am not rich, but I have a sound heart. We will do our beſt, and you shall be contented."

He went at once to speak to his wife; and together, by means of a mattress taken from their own bed, they arranged a couch for me on the floor of a vaſt cupboard.

Cruel men, you who have poisoned my life, and, through countless horrors and foul actions—to be recorded presently—have in some sort isolated me from all nature! no doubt the picture of a simple and noble beneficence is torture to you. When I force you to hear my tale of woe, may your gangrened souls recall your persecutions: at leaſt, cease to ſtifle your remorse! To-day, when your illusions are deſtroyed, you muſt indeed feel remorse. Hearken thereto, judge yourselves, and foreſtall the condemnation which, if you do not seal lips ready to pronounce your names and your crimes to me, will be engraved on all hearts forthwith. Ah! I feel it: I ought to forget how slow, how tardy, was this juſtice; and my soul, sensible to pity for your present ſtate, should allow you to flee from your country in peace; surrendering readily to

public execration the task of punishing you and of
avenging me.

Since I muſt necessarily have been a heavy burden
on my worthy hoſt, his conduct was the more generous;
his lodging was nothing but a cellar, divided by a
partition: in the one half, which he called a room,
his bed ſtood, also a large table and a counter; the other
served as a kitchen—a space accommodating Teerhooſt
and his wife, a young girl of twenty, a jeweller, an
apothecary always drunk, and myself.

Teerhooſt, not content to feed and to lodge me,
tried also to divert my thoughts, taking me to taverns
and to public places, where, he conjectured, I ought to
find some pleasure. All these efforts were a boon
valued keenly by me, yet they were impotent to dispel
my sorrow. The moſt grievous and burdensome
sentiment agitating me was a memory of the unhappy
D'Alègre: I could not doubt that our merciless tor-
mentor had flung him into chains once more; and I
waited impatiently for some help from my father which
might furnish the means of plucking my friend thence;
for, out of the depths of my retreat, I was resolved at
leaſt to attempt all things suggeſted by my indignation
to the attainment of this end.

I met a very rich fellow fortuitously, a native of
Montagnac, my own birthplace: he did not know me
personally, having lived in Amſterdam for a considerable time; but he well remembered my father and all
my family. He, quite different from M. Martin,
overwhelmed me with civilities and indulgence. He
insiſted on my going to lodge with him; he gave me a
place at his table, a room; also linen, of which I had had
no change for over forty days; and he had a pleasing
suit of clothes made for me. This honeſt Frenchman,
Louis Clergue, akin to Teerhooſt in his goodness and
sensibility, took a similar intereſt in my plight, and
offered services equally touching though more effective

in relief. He kept exceeding good company, and, as soon as he heard a full account of my misfortunes, assembled all his friends, less to give information and to satisfy their curiosity than to ease his own mind and to gather opinions concerning the course I ought to pursue. The kidnapping of D'Alègre at Brussels acutely alarmed him in its relation to me, and instructed him in the anger and the influence of the Marquise de Pompadour; and he feared she might take steps against me in Holland, as she had taken steps against my companion in Brabant.

Everybody thought I ran no risk, and that the States General and the people of Amsterdam would not so foully betray the confidence I showed in coming to seek shelter and protection among them; everybody advised me here quietly to enjoy the peace I had found.

The honest M. Clergue, however, was not reassured. He suspected that shame might have prevented my owning faults committed, since he could not imagine such a scandalous persecution of an innocent man, and, proceeding from this idea, he could only believe me guilty of serious offences. One day he took me aside, and said:

" Perhaps you have been led astray by high passions, or by inadvertence, so falling into excesses. Sometimes even an innocent mind feels remorse. I will not try to read into your mind. Consult yourself, and if you blame yourself for anything, I can procure the means whereby you may reach a place where you will be sheltered from all fear. To-morrow I will invite a ship's captain to sup with you. He is about to leave for Surinam, and I can easily persuade him to take you on board."

I assured him that I had told the strict truth, having absolutely nothing wherewith to reproach myself; that, strong in my innocence, I fancied I could defy the rage of my persecutors.

This I believed; yet, even as I thus deceived myself, they were contriving a vile plot against me. The French Ambassador demeaned himself, soliciting permission from the Dutch States to have me arrested; and this haughty Senate, intimidated by threats or corrupted by a little gold,* were cowardly enough to comply. All my movements were watched so closely that, despite the precautions I had taken of changing my name and of having no letters addressed directly to me, these letters were intercepted, one alone being allowed to reach me; and it furnished the means of my capture. The danger of arresting me in M. Clergue's house may be readily conceived; for, in my defence, he had interested a people vain of their freedom; and explanations of the motives wherefore mine was to be ravished from me would certainly be demanded. The following means were taken to avoid this difficulty. The letter from my father, permitted to reach me, enclosed a bill on a M. Marc Fraissinet, an Amsterdam banker—a bill made payable on June 1st of this year, 1756. On that day my steps were dogged everywhere; and at ten o'clock in the morning, when I presented myself at the banker's, I was arrested, bound, and dragged ignominiously into the thick of a greedy populace, who were made to believe that I was a notorious scoundrel. The crowd, attracted by this spectacle, quickly became so considerable that we could not stir; the bailiff's men—called *dindres* in this country—escorting me, armed with stout staves, belaboured those who surrounded us; and, needless to say, they gave the preference to me, so to hasten my steps. In this fashion they led me to the Town Hall. There we met such a mass of the curious that my *dindres* had to redouble their blows in order to make

* I found out later, and have seen proofs, that the French Government spent on this account two hundred and seventeen thousand livres. *Two hundred and seventeen thousand livres!*

way for me; and one blow fell so heavily on my neck that I dropped, unconscious. How long I remained in this state I do not know, nor in what manner I was brought out of the Town Hall; but I found myself alone when I recovered consciousness, having been flung on a little straw in a black dungeon. What a frightful awakening!—is there a mind keen enough to picture the full dread of such a thing? My imagination, long nurtured on gloomy and heart-corroding thoughts, seemed to collect all the weight at my heart to lacerate me. Once more I faced this terrible solitude, this death-like silence, one so often hitherto crushing my whole being; and now it seemed yet more horrible and oppressive. Formerly I had at least been sustained by hope, and even comforted in my chains: this time, no hope remained. Almighty God! . . . No hope remained! . . .

About nine o'clock I was visited by the French detective who had arrested me, one Saint-Marc. This miserable wretch came to insult me; he outraged me cruelly and basely with his insipid ironies. He said I ought only to pronounce the name of the Marquise de Pompadour with respect, since she was waiting to shower favours on me: instead of complaining, I should dutifully kiss the benign hand that struck me, each stroke being a kindness, a benefaction. . . . I did not deign reply to such a vile and despicable rascal.

Louis Clergue, however, and those of his friends who knew of my innocence, learned my fate, intrigued among the people, and began to excite them. I was informed of murmurs already to be heard, also that the citizens were demanding my freedom, boldly accusing the Government of violating the rights of the people and of hospitality, in my person, and that they dared to call for vengeance. This news gave sharp fright to me: I reflected that, since I was at the mercy of my enemies, and if they were forced to give an account of their deeds, it would be far more easy for them to make away with me and to spread a report— which no one would have interest enough in me to contradict—that I had been guilty of some great crime and sought by killing myself to escape from torture or from my own despair.

I had given myself wholly to this fear when I received a second visit from the police-officer Saint-Marc; who, after maliciously congratulating me on the hope I must have fancied of a near deliverance, told me he had brought an ounce of excellent snuff in order to set himself right with me. My suspicions will, no doubt, be understood; they seemed only too legitimate, though I know not whether they were well founded. Anyhow, at first, I took his gift impulsively, charged with these notions, regarding it as a boon; but I confess that other feelings succeeded to this frenzy. Is it therefore possible that, at such moments, life still has charms? And are the pleasures of existence so vivid that nothing can stifle the longing to enjoy them? I threw the snuff away; nor is it difficult to figure that my imagination, otherwise deeply impressed, was yet more harassed after this occurrence, and that I seemed to see proofs of assassination everywhere. When, on the morrow, my gaoler entered the cell, I thought I could detect surprise in his expression.

I endured a greater cruelty the next day. About eight o'clock in the evening I heard a loud noise and, on a sudden, caught sight through my dungeon-bars of eight or ten persons, some carrying lanterns, others pointed iron bars and enormous hammers. My door opened, and these fellows—whose faces alone would have inspired fear—surrounded me, without offering one single word. At once, on seeing their instruments, I tried to divine what the form of my torture must be, and what were the several functions of these brutes.

They appeared to regard me with attention for a lengthy time.

"Well!" I shouted at them. "Strike! I await your blows."

They did not reply. Some of them turned to examine the walls of my dungeon; and I fancied they were seeking a convenient spot in which to fix a nail and hang a cord. Others, with their iron bars, tested the stones, seeing if any were detached; and the rest struck at the gratings with their hammers. These operations completed, they all went away, and without having uttered a word.

I heard afterwards that this was an inspection of dungeons, and took place in this country at frequent intervals. I remained nine days in my cell, and had no word of anything; during which time solicitation had been made to the governor-general of Brabant for permission to pass me through the territory of the Empress—permission sure to be accorded by the man who, contrary to all law, had allowed the wretched D'Alègre to be kidnapped from under his very eyes. I would that I had been able to keep silent concerning this governor's name, and, above all, that I knew it not: I am deeply pained to pronounce the name of PRINCE CHARLES OF LORRAINE. Apparently nothing in relation to my affairs was sacred, and the most honest and generous minds betrayed themselves and lied to themselves when the question of harming me arose.

This fatal permission arrived; and, at ten o'clock in the morning of June 9th, 1756, a leathern belt, brought to my dungeon, was fastened around my body; two thick rings with padlocks were attached on each side, and my hands, thus confined, hung down and were held to my flanks. In consequence, and by a barbarous refinement, my treatment was more cruel than that suffered by unprincipled wretches, on whom only

7

handcuffs are fixed, so that they can move and use
their arms; whereas mine were immovable—a violence
and a torment inconceivable, unless experienced.
Then they put me in a sledge, together with a Dutch
police-officer, and a *dindre* at each door; and in this
plight, for the second time, I had to run the gauntlet
of the inhabitants of Amsterdam, who, deceived by a
report, supposed I must be one of those notorious
villains to whom no State could ever afford asylum.*

The French police-officer awaited me when I arrived
at the quay.   I embarked in a huge boat hired specially
to take me to Rotterdam, where we found another on
its way to Antwerp.   I could have forgiven my gaolers
for settling themselves comfortably on this boat; but,
since there was sufficient room to accommodate at
least two hundred persons, they might have put me in
a place where I could have been equally at ease: vilely
cruel, they threw me into a stinking, filthy corner, and
here the *dindres* were sent to eat with me; nor did they
deign to listen when I protested vainly against this
ignominy—hence I had to remain in the company of
a low rabble.   This was by no means all: the bonds
that encircled my arms did not permit me to raise my
hands to my mouth; consequently I had to be fed.
When I realized that I had to look to the service of
these men, revolting in their slovenliness, I refused to
take my nourishment, and for more than twenty-four
hours.   The next day, however, they used force, and
made me swallow food.   My *dindres* came with a

* Among the numerous infamies allowed against me, I must not
forget one they dared to inflict—that of rendering me no account of
the bill in sum-total I was to receive at Amsterdam, at Fraissinet's, nor
yet of one intercepted at Brussels.   I admit that at the Bastille I always
had the exact sum my father sent to me : M. de Cabanca, adjutant
of the guards, who received it from him, forwarded it to the lieutenant
of police.   Therefore I can only accuse the detective Saint-Marc of
theft ; and the sole detail he vouchsafed on the subject was an assurance
that he had paid my expenses due to Jean Teerhoost.

piece of beef swimming in sauce, took the meat in their fingers, and put it in my mouth; then, after dipping soft bread in the sauce, they made me gulp it in the same manner. In the midst of this cruel performance, one of these fellows blew his nose, using his fingers: and, without wiping them, he soaked the bread and advanced to place it between my lips. I turned my head aside, yet too late: I had seen the preliminaries, and my gorge rose violently. I suffered a prolonged and a dreadful sickness, which left me weak and immobile. When I came to myself, I begged as a favour that irons might be put on my hands and feet, so that I could be free from the fatal belt; and no doubt I should have pleaded in vain, but for a servant of the French police-officer, who, touched to tears by my frightful position, raised his voice against such barbarity, and, drawing his knife, said he would cut the infamous bonds himself if I were not freed from them. An account of his protests, and of my plaints, was carried to the police-officer; who, at that moment, was enlivening his tedium with a woman he had brought from Paris, this woman also serving him as spy. He ordered that new fetters should be brought to replace those I wore: my belt was removed and a handcuff fastened on my right arm, separated by a chain of about a foot in length from another attached to the left arm of one of my *dindres*, at whose mercy I thus found myself, and in such sort that one could not make a motion without involving the other or drawing his attention. When we reached the harbour at Rotterdam, my infernal belt was replaced; and we crossed the town through the thick of an assembled crowd, which accompanied me as far as the quay. Now they carried me to the lowest depth of the hold in a boat destined to take us to Antwerp. There we were awaited by the grand-provost of Brabant and three archers; and the latter mounted with us in post-chaises. My arms were tied behind me, and thus we were conducted as far as Lille.

When we arrived, the police-officer escorting me dismissed the satellites who had followed us; and, judging fit to rest from his fatigues in this town, he took me to the royal prison, where he insisted that the gaoler should guarantee my person. This fellow, for greater security, took it into his head to fasten me with a screw-bolt to the chain of a deserter, who, on his way to his regiment, had received warning that he would be hanged the next day. This miserable young man was barely nineteen years old. The sort of night we passed can be easily pictured: my cheerless companion tried to persuade me that I too would undoubtedly be hanged; and his most minor project involved the making of ropes from our shirts, with which to strangle ourselves in company.

Such were our meditations when they fetched me to continue the route on the morrow. The detective Saint-Marc, after the precaution of having my feet put in irons, took his place in the post-chaise beside me. He was armed with pistols, likewise his servant, who ran near the door, and with orders to shoot me if I made the slightest movement; but surely this would not have alarmed me greatly, even if I had been able to move.

Thus we arrived at the Bastille about ten o'clock on the morning of the next day. Saint-Marc had the welcome of a benevolent divinity: all the officers of the prison rushed to meet him, thus, by a thronged retinue, to make his progress more imposing, his reception more illustrious. They congratulated and enbraced him, they lauded his efforts and sympathized with his hardships, each one seeming eager to compensate him by some delicate attention. As for me!— I was despoiled of my clothing and covered with rags half-rotted, as formerly; irons were placed on my hands

PLATE IV

THE BASTILLE BEFORE ITS DEMOLITION

[face p. 100

and feet, and I was thrown anew on to a heap of straw in a dungeon. Here, for warders, I had all the fellows from whose surveillance I had escaped, and who had been punished by a three months' imprisonment for the crime of having failed to prevent my evasion.

I will not weary the imagination of my readers by a new description of my fearsome plight; they will divine this readily, and without any need of my awakening and tiring their sensibilities once more.

I remained in irons for forty consecutive months, a prey to all the abominations of my fate and to the tyranny of my ruthless tormentors.

I shall refer elsewhere to the report of the surgeon commissioned to give an account of my condition: indeed, the story of all I suffered at that time is enough to make one's flesh crawl. However, enough has been said for the present about tortures and torturers, so let us turn for a moment to the consolations, even the alleviations, I enjoyed in this dungeon.

Yes, I managed to find alleviations! This, as may be easily imagined, was not at the hands of men: how could I expect anything of the sort from them? I found relief in the company of animals seemingly the most loathsome and repulsive to us—and this by taking part in their play and pleasures, and, I might add, by inducing them to love me. Gentle readers, whose generous and tender hearts understand and wholly share my feelings, will readily excuse the details I am about to proffer. Ah! probably you, like myself, and in your anger at so much cruelty, have felt the necessity of escaping from the regard of men and of soothing yourselves with animals.

For a long time I had counted as part of my physical miseries the disgust of being annoyed incessantly by a crowd of rats as they came to find shelter and pasture in my straw. Sometimes when I slept they ran over my face, and frequently they inflicted severe pain by biting me. I was helpless to deliver myself from their capers, forced to live with them; and I conceived the plan of fraternizing with them. In a little time they deigned to admit me among themselves, and it is to them that I owe the solitary, pleasurable distraction experienced throughout the thirty-five years of my pain. I must show how we formed and established this interesting partnership.

Bastille dungeons are octagonal; and the one in which I lay had a loophole two and a half feet above the floor, an opening about two feet long and eighteen inches wide, diminishing gradually; hence, at the outer dungeon wall, it measured scarcely more than three inches. The slight amount of air and daylight possible for my enjoyment came thence; and the stone forming the base served as a seat and a table when, weary with lying on putrid straw, I dragged myself to this loophole to breathe fresh air; and I could support my elbows and my arms on this horizontal stone, so reducing the weight of my fetters. One day, whilst in this attitude, I saw a great rat appear at the far extremity of the loophole. I called to him; he looked at me boldly; and I threw a morsel of bread to him gently, using care so that I should not startle him by a sudden movement. He advanced, took the morsel, withdrew a little to eat it, and appeared to demand a second piece from me; which I threw to him, yet nearer to me; and a third, nearer still, and so with others. This performance continued as long as I had bread to give to him; and he, after having satisfied his appetite, stored the remaining small pieces in a hole.

The next day he came again, and I proved equally liberal; I even added some meat, which he appeared to like better than the bread; and this time he ate it in my presence, as he had not done on the previous evening. He was familiar enough by the third day to take what I offered from my fingers.

I did not know where his former dwelling might be, but he seemed willing to change it and to come nearer to me. He spied a moderately deep hole on each side of the loophole, went to examine them, and set up house in the one on the right, apparently the most commodious to him. Here he slept for the first time on the fifth day. The following day he came to call on me quite early in the morning, and I gave him his breakfast; and when he had eaten, he left me, nor did I see him again until the next day, when he arrived as usual. As he came from the hole I saw that he was not alone, noticing a female, who displayed her head only and seemed to be watching our doings together. I called, without effect, and threw bread and meat to her; but she appeared excessively timid and did not at once advance to take the food. However, by degrees she ventured from the hole and took the morsels I had placed in the middle of the track; and occasionally she disputed with the male, and, when she had proved more strong and cunning than he, she fled to her retreat, carrying whatever she had seized. Consequently the first rat came nearer to me, for consolation; and, to punish her, he ate all I gave to him, and at a distance far enough from the hole to prevent her daring to come and dispute possession; yet invariably he affected to show the food, so to brave her. Then he sat himself on his haunches, held the bread or the meat with his forepaws, like a monkey, and nibbled it proudly. One day, however, the female's vanity having doubtless overcome her discretion, she darted out and managed to grasp a morsel with her teeth; meanwhile, the male clung to it with his teeth; neither one nor the other would let go; and in this fashion they descended into the hole, the female, in advance, dragging the male after her.

What a contrast this touching sight made with my troubles and recollections! In the thick of the world and its agitations one can hardly conceive the possibility of giving attention to like pleasures or deriving rapture therefrom. No, I am wrong; for those who can retreat into themselves on occasion and discover the sensitive mind will appreciate a joy similar to mine and understand its charm with me. But let us leave all distracting reflections and hasten to rejoin my innocent and lovable companions.

Immediately my dinner came, I called to them. The male ran to me; and the female, as usual, approached slowly and timorously. At last, however, she decided to come nearer to me, and thenceforward she grew accustomed to eat from my hand. Later, a third rat presented himself, one who stood less on ceremony and became part of the family after his second visit; and, seemingly, his pleasure was such that he wanted his comrades to share my friendship and favours, for, the next day, he came with two others; and they, during the week, brought five more. Thus, in less than a fortnight, our society comprised ten stout rats and myself.

I gave each one a name, which, in a little time, they could remember, recognizing themselves when I called, advancing to eat with me from the dish or from my plate; but such freedom displeased me, and I was forced to set their table apart, to avoid their dirt.

I had tamed them to such an extent that they seemed to find pleasure in letting me scratch them under the throat; but never would they allow me to touch their backs. Sometimes I amused myself by making them play and by playing with them; now I threw a very hot piece to them, and the most precipitate fell on it, burned themselves, squealed, and dropped it, while the less greedy, having waited, took the cooled fragment, fled to a corner, and shared it. Again, I held bread or meat suspended, and they had to jump for it. I had named one of the females Rapino-swallow,

because of her great agility, and I was encl
habituating her to this kind of exercise; for, s
her superiority over the others, she scorned to
herself on anything I gave to them, took the
position of a dog pointing at game, allowed a ra
jump in pursuit of the morsel; and, just as he reac
it, up she sprang and seized it with her jaws in the air.
Woe to him if she did not succeed; for then, and
without fail, she gripped him by the neck and bit at
him with her needle-sharp teeth until the pain made
him shriek and drop his booty, whereupon Rapino-
swallow darted away, and he retired elsewhere to cure
himself of wounds inflicted by her.

Thus for almost two years I was luckily able to
lighten my harsh miseries with these simple and
innocent frolics. Several times I thought to surprise
myself in a momentary enjoyment: a beneficent God
no doubt created this new charm, at which my imagination seemed to yield promptly and without effort.
In these happy moments the world ceased to exist for
me. The memory of men and of their savagery,
recalled to mind at such times, emerged only as in a
dream. My intellectual horizon was limited by the
walls of the dungeon; my senses, soul, and spirit, were
concentrated therein; I found myself in the bosom of
a family, interesting me and loving me. Why trans-
port myself to other spheres, where I should discover
nothing but tormentors and assassins?

But alas! this gentle, kindly mode of life did not
always sustain my courage; and then I had to pay
dearly for such a precious surrender, such a forgetfulness of care. Notwithstanding, by a happy chance,
new means were provided to delude my mind and to
furnish variety in the gambols of my pupils, doubling
my entertainment.

One day, when my straw was about to be changed,
I noticed a piece of elder used as a bind for the new

supply. This discovery gave me an inexpressible emotion: promptly the idea of making a flageolet flashed into my mind and filled me with delight. Until this moment I had heard no sound in my dungeon except the clang of bolts and chains: henceforward I could dissipate this terror with soft and soothing melodies; and, anyhow, I could make a cadence of my sighs, perhaps by this means shortening the painful slow hours of misery and alluring my griefs and easing my pains. What an abundant source of joy! But how make the flageolet! My hands were fast in two thick iron rings fixed by a bar of the same metal, and—let it be remembered—if in effect I could move them, this meant prodigious difficulty; moreover, I had no tools. My gaolers would not have given me as much as a piece of wood; no, not even for riches! I bethought myself of detaching the buckle that fastened my breeches-belt: my foot-irons served to prepare it, to bend it, making a sort of small scissors; but they were fragile, and only after great trouble could I manage to sever and to withdraw the pith, fashioning the elder. Finally, after months of labour and trial, this boon materialized: I say boon, for, as one may suppose, it proved genuine; and each day I rejoiced, and my interest quickened. I have possessed this little instrument for thirty-four years; never for a moment have I been without it during thirty-four years. Long has it solaced my pains, and it enlivens my pleasure to-day. I shall take care that it must pass at my death—after having served to embellish the last days of my life—into the hands of an apostle of liberty; and therefore, placed subsequently in one of her temples, it may recall the crimes of despotism, together with innumerable memorials.

The time necessarily spent on this important work had distracted me in some measure from my domestic cares, and I had neglected my little family, which during this interval had much increased, numbering twenty-six in less than a year. I felt that here were no strangers, those who sought to intrude being ill-received and forced to fight at the outset. These combats amused me greatly. When the two champions were face to face they appeared to judge their respective strengths at a first glance, even before trial; then the stronger gnashed his teeth, and the weaker began to squeal and to retreat backward, and without turning, otherwise his adversary might have leapt on his back and bitten him. The stronger makes no frontal attack, since in so doing he would expose himself to the loss of his eyes. His method of procedure is ingenious and entertaining: he puts his head between his forepaws, turns two or three somersaults until the middle of his back comes in contact with his enemy's snout; and, the latter trying thereupon to escape, the first chooses the moment to pounce on him, clinging to him, and they may fight desperately; meanwhile, if other rats are present, they watch the struggle, never fighting two to one.

I have noticed one important fact—namely, that these animals seem frigid, rarely prone to love-heat. I have scrutinized them with the most close attention, have passed many a night in watching them, yet never have I been able to see them couple; but, in these matters, I made at least one observation, which seems curious. When a rat appears to be the victor in a love-fight, he limits his triumph to remaining firm on his legs, awaiting the female in this fashion; and she gives two or three cries, drags herself on her belly, places herself between the fore-paws of the male, who then urinates on her back.

I submit these divers remarks to more enlightened observers, and willingly leave them to their censure.

I wish I could have tamed spiders in the same way: but I was not so cunning as the unfortunate Pelisson. I thought of a rare method for catching them: I bound a fly with one of my hairs, suspended it over a hole where I knew a spider lay in wait; and when it came out and seized the fly, I pulled this way and that, and the spider, unable either to run up the hair or to detach itself from the fly, remained in my power.

Then I tied the hair to a grating and put a goblet full of water underneath. The spider let down a thread for descent, then, touching the water, immediately clambered again to the fly; and by this means I kept the spider for a lengthy time, though, try as I did, I failed to familiarize a single one.

I have prolonged these consoling tales as long as possible, even as in my captivity I prolonged the blessed distractions they recall to memory; for they helped me to lose sight of, though not entirely to forget, men; whom sometimes I remembered, likewise their cruelties and my miseries. Then I needed fresh distractions; and one, highly potent, arose in my mind, and I seized on the notion impetuously.

My active and impulsive mind has invariably evinced the need for conceiving and acting; free, and master of my faculties, I should have directed my ardours to useful channels; enchained, they served only to devise a means for the breaking of my fetters. Now I fancied I had lighted on a project which might fulfil one and the other aim; anyhow, I dared to flatter myself that if I rendered a service to the country, my liberty would be the reward. The following is the subject of my plan.

Long ago I had been struck by noticing that, among the troops, the officers and sergeants were armed solely with halberds, hence the courage of those bearing them was rendered useless during the greater part of a fight, and sometimes throughout a fight. The inconveniences of this usage were very numerous. In battle, side-arms are not always employed, or they are not employed until a late moment of the day; therefore, up to such a moment, what could the inferior officers do with their pikes and halberds? Yet they form more than a twentieth of the army, and are generally, in effect, the pick of it. No doubt a sergeant, whose grade denotes service and bravery, handles a musket better—and with more advantage to us and loss to the enemy—than a raw recruit, or an unpractised soldier who, troubled and scared by the frightful sight of slaughter, merely fires a useless musket-shot and with an unskilled hand. How was it possible that no one had thought of correcting such an absurdity, or of how much advantage in the first battle fought by France we should derive from the new arrangement I intended to sketch out, together with details showing the accompanying conveniences? How proud we might be in giving simultaneously a lesson, and an example of this method, to the heroes of Prussia!

I was teased by the desire to communicate these notions to my King and to the minister of war; notions that, imperatively, must not be divulged before my plans were realized and put into execution. But how write them down, how succeed in transferring them from my mind to the cognizance of others? During my first detention, M. Berryer had taken on himself to recommend that ink and paper should be given to me; this time, however, I was deprived of that luxury, direct orders having been given to prevent my enjoying such things. Once again I must take counsel with my head and, I say boldly, with my courage and industry, so to find means wherewith to write down the project, though I had neither pens nor paper. I contrived the matter thus:

As substitute for the paper I lacked I took crumbs from my ration of bread, and so for a considerable period. I pounded them in my hands and kneaded them with saliva; then, by pressure, I made tablets six inches square, or thereabouts, and a sixth of an inch thick. (Anyone can try this experiment, and he will find that these tablets, if necessary, take the place of paper.) In default of pens I took one of the triangular bones discoverable under the belly of a carp: these bones are broad, strong, and, when split, may be used easily instead of pens. Ink was all I wanted now; but my blood could supply the deficiency, and my blood I used. I drew threads from the lappet of my shirt; I bound the first joint of my thumb firmly, so to make the extremity swell, and this I pierced with the tongue of one of my buckles; but each prick furnished only a few drops of blood; and they had to be renewed frequently, so that all my fingers were soon covered with wounds causing a swelling and much irritation, of which I feared the consequence. In addition, my blood congealed as I wrote each letter, and I was obliged to dip my pen anew. To remedy these two defects, I ran sundry drops of my blood into a small quantity of water at the bottom of my goblet; and this mixture provided a smooth ink, with which I managed to write quite legibly a memorandum giving in detail all the notions set forth above.

This, however, was not enough. My memorandum must be copied fair and written on paper for presentation to the minister; and I could not expect this service from any of my gaolers, nor from the officers of the Bastille; for either they would have broken my tablets, or they might have appropriated my work, taking the honour of the project to themselves. Meanwhile, no one ever came near to me, except a turnkey who had the right of entry to my tomb. Once more I had to use stratagem. I asked to see the major; and in spite of the feeble desires of these gentlemen to comply with the wishes of prisoners, I spoke firmly enough to oblige him not to keep me waiting over long. When he entered my dungeon I asked him whether it was the Marquise de Pompadour's intention to send me body and soul to the devil. I said to him:

"You see, I cannot hope much longer to resist the frightful torments I suffer. I demand that I be given the grace never yet withheld even from the greatest scoundrels."

He promised that this should not be refused, and he would send the Bastille confessor to me forthwith; for it ought to be known that this office was a charge on the place, and the priest who fulfilled the function was an officer of the staff, one of its tools, above all one of its spies, in consequence. Thus, in this foul den where nothing was sacred, they did not fear to profane our most holy mysteries; they found ministers of the God of Peace who were base enough to prostitute their august rights and barbarous enough to become the accomplices of so many horrors.

A Father Griffet occupied the position at this time —a Jesuit known to literature, in addition, by some estimable productions. He came, and, without concerning himself about the object wherefore I had apparently made my demand, without even mentioning the word *confession*, he asked a thousand questions touching the whole of my past life, my escapes, and the means I had used to achieve them. I tried to interest him deeply, and, when I thought I had succeeded, I mentioned my project, earnestly begging him to read it, and, if he approved, to procure me facilities for making it known. He consented; and at once I gave to him the six tablets whereon I had written. He seemed transported in a kind of admiration mingled with dread when he saw tablets stained by my blood. He said:

"Why haven't you a Cardinal de Richelieu or a King of Prussia for master? They would foster and reward your genius instead of stifling it in a dungeon."

I answered that our ministers had nothing but the

savage despotism of these two great men, together with
a cowardice arisen from impotence and an utter vacuity
of mind. Anyhow, our concern at the moment was
my project, which I read to him. He approved, and
promised at once to go and communicate it to the
lieutenant of police, and to solicit an order for ink
and paper whereby I could transcribe the writing and
put it in a state for presentation. He succeeded in
his request; I had everything I needed; and on the
14th of April, 1758, my memorandum was presented
to the King. Assuredly he read it; and, doubtless,
all my observations were effective, since they were put
into use without delay. At this period, and in accord-
ance with my plan, all the sergeants and inferior
officers in our regiments were armed with muskets,
the value of over twenty thousand good soldiers being
thus rendered more active and useful; a value, to all
intents and purposes, hitherto crippled.

If a grandee's or a courtesan's favourite had been
the author of this project, he would have had reward
with honours and large pensions; and would to God
such honours were allotted alone to those who so merited
them! As for myself, I only demanded the opportunity to be useful yet again and, on obtaining my
freedom, to be able to render new and more signal
services to my country. I did not know that, under
the reign of the Marquise de Pompadour, to beg for
deliverance by such methods meant a loading of chains
on myself and a more secure riveting of the bonds that
encompassed me. The greater the activity, and perhaps
the attainments, I showed, the more dangerous I
appeared to her. Probably she said, like Louis XI,
whose mind she might well know, whose feelings she
might well guess: *Rid me of this enemy, or he will snap
at me.* With such ideas she would be little disposed
to employ my zeal. But ought I to attribute such
motives to her? Could I believe specifically that she

alone held the thread to work all springs ? Alas! this
was only too true: she retained as ministers none save
those cowardly enough to fear her or base enough to
serve her.

After having vainly expected the desired price of
this service during three months, a price I had been
forced to beseech as a favour—though I had every
right to demand it in justice—I thought I might
attract the attention of the King and his ministers, and
rouse their consideration by submitting yet another
plan. The first was likely to cause bloodier battles for
our enemies: the object of the second was to alleviate
some of the evils arising therefrom among ourselves.

It seemed appalling to me that the widow of an officer
or of a soldier could shed nothing but sterile tears over
the ashes of a husband who had died for the sake of
his country; that the State, having caused her sorrow,
and usually her poverty, should not attempt to relieve
them. The King of Prussia had already conferred a
pension on all widows: and this act, attesting the just-
ness and tenderness of his heart, perhaps did more for
his fame than brilliant triumphs and skill in battle.
I had heard him lauded everywhere with enthusiasm,
and I yearned anxiously to see my King invested with
a like glory; but funds were necessary to this end.
(An indebted State could apparently provide for the
prodigalities of a mistress and the greed of courtiers,
but not for acts of justice and humanity.) I pointed
out a means whereby, and without encumbering the
people, every citizen would be in the position of
acquitting the debt personal to them all: this consisted
in raising the postage on all letters by three *deniers*.
I proved, at a minimum calculation, how this slight
tax, borne by all and to the overburdening of none,
would be more than sufficient. I indicated the details
of this arrangement and the facilities for assuring its
success.

8

I engaged the soul of the monarch to execute this noble, simple, and natural plan, reminding him that one merits happiness alone by giving happiness. His heart was formed to recognize such a truth, one worthy of his hearing if his mind, less compliant, had not surrendered to impressions foreign to him and imposed on him.

This time I was far from attaining the actual end I had in view; for, instead of serving and honouring the State, I had the misfortune to see new burdens heaped by the abuse of means indicated by me. Hardly had my memorandum been presented at Court when the postage on letters was, in fact, raised, under the pretext of obtaining money to pension the widows of soldiers and officers who had died fighting; but this pretext was an odious lie, deceiving the people: the ministers disposed of the tax-proceeds, and the widows had no recompense.

And I—could I no longer hope? None of the cries uttered from the depth of my prison would be listened to again, either because they recalled my innocence and my pains, or because they bore witness to my services— at least to my wish, and power, to render service to my country. Already I had been incarcerated for nine years, persecuted, loaded with shameful fetters, nor had I yet learned my crime: no accuser, no witness, had been produced against me; I had confronted no judge. I invoked the laws, and they were dumb, their ministers being deaf to my plaints. Citizens, thus they trifle with your lives! A vile prostitute, her very lackeys— or your ministers so often fit for naught save lackey-dom—could open or shut these frightful doors on you at will; passions alone were their guides; their only judge was a worn-out conscience, become incapable alike of remorse or of energy in crime.

Did these foolish despots indeed fancy you would eternally and respectfully kiss the infamous chains

enfettering you, because you were bowed under the
yoke by habit? Imbeciles! They did not realize
that in overweighting the chains they were inciting
you to revolt, teaching you to know yourselves; they
could not see that they themselves were augmenting
the clouds above their heads whence the thunderbolt
would fall to shatter them.

Accordingly I could not further allure myself with
hopes of an end to my wretchedness; this straw,
drenched for so long by my tears, would prove to be
my grave. Clemency, justice, pity—I implored them
all in vain. What name can be used to qualify this
appalling despotism? If it be true, as a famous writer
said (*The Friend of Men*, Vol. VI, p. 72): "Judgments
without law and without appeal are a prerogative which
would degenerate into tyranny in the actual hand of
Equity itself, if Equity did not recoil with horror at
such practice"—if this be true, how name these
lawless acts? For no one even stooped to make them
judicial, and they were committed with impunity at
the beck of the most despicable of men or of women,
whose mere names outraged morals and revolted
decency. Such were the shameful assaults whereof
so many men in France have been the victims; acts
dishonourable to every fellow-citizen base enough to
permit them and witless enough not to fear them.

I was reduced to that foul pass when a wretched
man, whom nothing sustains—mistaking the laws which
betray him, no longer hearing the voice of conscience—
puts crime in the rank of duty. Yes, I will own it.
My hand, misled by despair, braved an attempt to
hasten the moment that would make an end to my woes.
I do not pretend to justify this fault; but who can at
least refrain from pitying me, while yet accusing me?
I ask no further reference to myself in the estimate of
my torments: a notion of them shall be given by an
irreproachable witness. Among the papers relative

to my imprisonment, handed to me at the Baſtille on
July 16th laſt, was the report I am about to quote from
a surgeon commissioned by M. de Sartine to visit me
and to give an account of my condition. Hear him.
This man, if he is honeſt, merits full belief; if not, it
would be difficult to accuse him of pretending to
impute to despotism crimes for which it was not
responsible. Anyhow, he cannot be suspeċted.

" SIR,
        " In accord with your orders, several
times I have been to see a prisoner at the Baſtille;
and after having examined his eyes, and pondered
deeply over all this prisoner has told to me, I do
not think it extraordinary that, to a great extent,
he should have damaged his sight. During
many years the prisoner has been deprived of air
and the effeċt of the sun. He has been in a
dungeon for forty months, and with irons on his
feet and hands. Nature suffers in a like situation.
It is impossible to avoid weeping over such great
misfortunes: if an excessive salivation weakens
the lungs, even the whole body, there is no doubt
that too profuse an abundance of tears, shed
during so long a period, muſt have contributed
to exhauſt the sight of this prisoner.
        " The winter of 1756-1757 was extremely
severe, and the Seine was frozen, as in the previous
winter. Exaċtly at this time the prisoner, ironed
foot and hand, lay on ſtraw in his dungeon, and
without blankets: in this place there were two
loopholes five inches wide, about five feet high,
and having neither glass nor panels to close them.
Day and night the cold and the wind beat on his
face; nor is anything so harmful to the sight
as an icy wind, particularly at a time of sleep.
The mucus from his nose caused his upper lip to

split as far as the nostril, thus the teeth were
exposed, and the cold cracked them; the roots
of his whiskers were seared by the cold; he
became bald. I have examined these four parts
with close attention, and traces are even now
quite perceptible.

"Thus the cold cracked his teeth and split
his upper lip as far as the nose and seared the hair
of his whiskers at the roots and caused baldness;
and there is no doubt that his eyes, infinitely more
delicate and susceptible to impression than the
four parts mentioned above, have suffered yet
more severely, and have undergone a similar
decay.

"There are four iron gratings over the prisoner's window; the bars are very thick, crossed
in such a manner that when one wishes to look at
a single object, one sees thirty of the same: this,
in time, severs the visual rays, and is exceedingly
bad for the sight. The walls of the Bastille
being nine feet or ten feet thick, the rooms must
be very damp in consequence; and damp relaxes
all parts of the body and reduces the vital and
animal spirits.

"The prisoner, unable to endure his miseries,
resolved to take his own life: to this end, he
remained one hundred and thirty-three hours
without eating or drinking. His mouth was
opened by means of keys, and he had to swallow
nourishment, given by force. He found himself
recalled to life, in spite of himself; and he took
a piece of glass, cut four of his veins, and lost
most of his blood during the night, so that barely
six ounces remained in him. He was unconscious
for several days: the great loss of blood exhausted
his strength and enervated all his senses; and
although the prisoner has regained a certain

stoutness, his health cannot be judged by this, for—his blood having been exhausted—he has not sufficient heat or enough strength to throw off humours by transpiration. These humours coagulate, congeal, and form a kind of fat, provoking all sorts of illnesses; for we discover that very fat people are oppressed by rheumatism, together with obstructions, ulcers, gout; and these arise solely from exhaustion and a faulty transpiration. The prisoner also complains of rheumatism and other infirmities, these likewise contracted in the dungeon; but I do not mention such diseases, since they are not within my province.*

" Now the chief cause of his failing of sight arises from his exhausted blood: this is proved in an endless number of persons who complain of short or feeble sight; and they say that the evil has been caused by excessive bleeding to cure other maladies suffered by them.

" This prisoner complains that his sight is very dim, and diminishes constantly. The man is no longer young, and has passed middle-age, being forty-two: he has endured harsh ordeals. He has now suffered for fifteen years without intermission: for seven years he has been deprived of fire, light, air, and sunshine; furthermore, as I said above, he has been fifty-eight months in the dungeons and forty months with irons on his feet and hands, and lying on straw without blankets.

" Assuredly, in such situations, nature exhausts itself by dint of weeping and misery. When the prisoner bends his head forward, or if he is reading or writing, he feels concussions in the upper part of the brain, as if struck by heavy fist-blows; and, simultaneously, he loses his sight, and for two or three minutes. This is caused by a too

* M. Dejean, the writer of this letter, was only a surgeon-oculist.

great abundance of humours; the parts, having
loſt elaſticity, give way near the eye-cavity and
arreſt the return of blood from the optic vein,
which swells and compresses the optic nerve.
This causes him to lose his sight until the humours
have resumed their course. The latter symptom
is moſt dangerous; and it is much to be feared
that these convulsions may cause congeſtion in
the optic nerve, or a rupture of the vessels, which
might provoke apoplexy or paralysis of the
optic nerves.

"With eye-salves, balms, hot compound
washes and aromatic fumigations, I have entirely
arreſted the involuntary flow of tears and have
thoroughly reduced the inflammation of his eyes:
I have even succeeded in giving the original
elaſticity to the orbicular muscles of the iris,
which were greatly dilated. This would have
reſtored his sight to a proper condition, if the
diminution had been caused by these two symp-
toms alone; but, since his loss of sight arises from
an exhauſtion of tears and blood, there is no
possibility of reſtoring that sight. Sir, I have
thought it essential to give this account to you,
because it is useless to spend the King's money
on remedies or on my visits; for nothing but
air, much exercise, and the cessation of misery,
can retain the small measure of sight yet left to
the prisoner. The air will ſtrengthen all parts
of his body, and proper exercise will dissipate
the excessive quantity of humours in his head,
which cause the frequent convulsions and, if his
torment continues, muſt lead to blindness.

"(*Signed*) DEJEAN."

The blood runs cold at the tale of such crimes; but
what new sentiment will be experienced when it

becomes known that the salutary counsels of this surgeon and the dreadful description he gave of my plight made no impression on the mind of my persecutors, and so I remained in my dungeon. I was not taken thence until long afterwards, when an overflowing of the Seine filled the place with water. Now let no one do my tormentors the honour of believing that pity inspired this action. Orders were given to remove me to one of the towers, solely because the turnkey who served me was obliged to wade through water each time he came, and protested vigorously.

At last I breathed a clearer air and could see the heavens more distinctly. They put me in the first room of the tower named the County Tower; and since there was no fireplace, obviously, it much resembled a dungeon. Doubtless they were afraid to habituate my mind over-quickly to mitigations. Another reason for placing me in this room was derived from its position in the department of one named Daragon, the most pitiless of all men; who, having already been punished on account of me, and for not preventing my escape, would certainly not fail to persecute me the more cruelly under a pretext of guarding me more closely. Let me not be accused of imposing such atrocious motives on my enemies: readers who have followed all the actions of these men will not so reproach me, and may easily find the proof of my assertions in the knowledge they have gained of the feelings animating such persecutors: this will be a guide, leading them infallibly from cause to effect—even as a clever mechanic readily judges the force of resistance and the power of levers by seeing their effect on the mass they set in motion.

But what am I saying? I spoke of proofs. Ah! if proof be needed, this I can supply; and it will make one shudder.

I have said that, in many respects, my new dwelling

resembled the dungeon I had quitted but recently. The room was less damp, and the air I breathed less thick, or, rather, only unhealthy in my room; whereas, in the dungeon, it was so poisonous that I felt the cruel effects, and at each breath, in excruciating and profound pains. Such was the difference, no doubt considerable; but I had lost the distractions from and consolations in torment, for I had been unable to bring my little family with me. However, as I was regretting this fact bitterly, a happy chance offered a means of redress.

Pigeons came frequently to perch at my window. I conceived the plan of taming some of them; and probably, if I succeeded, they would promptly console me for the loss of my rats: their caresses would be more sweet, their friendship more touching! I sought to practise the ensuing notions, my mind being directed wholly to this end. I made a slight net with threads drawn from my shirts and sheets, held it outside my window, and so caught a superb male. Soon after I likewise took the female, who seemed anxious to share the bondage of her mate. I spared no pains to soothe them in their captivity; I helped them to make their nest, and to warm and nourish their young: my cares and tenderness equalled their own. They seemed sensible of this, and strove to repay me by tokens of affection. When this touching reciprocity of feeling had been established between us, I thought only of them. How I watched their movements! How I rejoiced in their love-making! I was lost to myself when near to them, and sometimes I dreamed of their fancied delights.

All the officials at the Bastille came to see this sight, amazed by my skill. I amused myself with their astonishment, speaking of the pleasure I derived; which they could scarcely imagine, such feelings being outside their capacities. Daragon, jealous, resolved to spoil my delight; for this fellow shook with rage if he thought that one throb of my heart was not a torture. A few of his superiors upheld him, and authorized all his infamies, since he was their pander and creature; and the liberties he dared to take won their approval. Accordingly he decided to rob me of my pigeons or to make me pay dearly for permission to keep them. Each Sunday I gave him one of the seven bottles of wine allowed to me for the week; and he had the impudence to demand four. I explained how impossible it muſt be in my weakness to shed myself of a relief so needful to suſtain and to reanimate my ſtrength. He replied that, otherwise, he would buy no more grain for my pigeons, even though I should pay four times its worth to him. I answered firmly, incensed by such impertinences. He went out, foaming in his anger; and he returned presently, saying he came in obedience to the governor, who had given the command to kill my pigeons. My despair at this pronouncement was extreme, upsetting my reason completely; and I would have given my life in order to slake a too legitimate vengeance on this monſter. I saw him make a move to fall on the innocent victims of my misfortune; I sprang forward to foreſtall him, seized them, and, in my frenzy, crushed them myself.

This moment was perhaps the moſt poignant of my life, nor can I ever recall the thought of it without anguish. I could not touch food for several days; pain and indignation warred in my mind; my sighs were shrieks and I loathed mankind.

Soon after we had a new governor, and this change brought about a change in our fate. The Count de Jumilhac, made to honour such a place, was generous and compassionate, giving thought to his prisoners, ever concerned to soften and to calm their woes. He seemed impressed by mine, promising to watch over me; and, in accord with his usual habits, he proved better than his word.

He procured an audience for me with the lieutenant of police, at that time M. de Sartine, who now appears on the stage, and will play a leading part in the history of my life henceforward.

He listened attentively to my statement, and my military plan especially greatly impressed him; he assured me that as soon as I had obtained my freedom he would see that the just reward merited by this service should be granted to me. He gave his word in the presence of the governor; of the Sieur Ferrant, King's lieutenant; and of M. Chevalier, major, who is still alive. Moreover, he assented to my being allowed to walk for two hours each day on the summit of the towers or along the Bastille platform.

My feelings toward this magistrate have corresponded in degree with the rulings of his conduct to me. To begin with he procured me the favour whereof I have spoken above. He seemed to regard me with some interest; and I showed my gratitude and sought to prove it by evincing confidence enough in him to submit for his observation two new plans already conceived.

The first related to the finances. At that time, as to-day, they were exhausted, in a state of confusion; unquestionably, we lacked cash. How proud I have been in these latter days to realize that the foundations on which I relied were identical with those employed as a base for the new financial plan decreed recently by the National Assembly. This has sanctioned and legalized the temporary issue of paper money. I proposed that coinage should serve a like purpose, destined to the same end, and to be withdrawn by similar means. The inconveniences which could be opposed to my plan squared with those put forward for the rejection of the new institution: in response,

I used precisely the same solutions as those offered by the Assembly to support their system. Here lies the proof of my plan, written at that period, and since read by a host of distinguished persons, who can testify to the fact.

The second project, taken forcibly from me by the commissary Chesnon on July 17th, 1777, aimed to establish public granaries, and, within the State, to prevent the dreadful troubles entailed by the mere idea of famine. Nothing could be more simple than the method I pointed out for the construction and the provisioning of these storehouses. This was the levying a light tax on marriages, one not compulsory, but which all rich folk, or those wishing to appear rich, would certainly and readily have paid; for I had cunningly based the scheme on vanity. It would be difficult to imagine the amazing results I reached through my natural and easy calculations: how many useful, neglected, or disregarded truths thus emerged startlingly from the simplest comparisons! I pointed out a sure method with which to shelter every province, city, market-town, and village in France from need, if there should be a corn-famine. What would we not owe to such establishments, especially to-day when the fury of our enemies dares to attempt the execrable plan of starving us, of rendering nature's bounties useless, so to force the people in an access of despair to shatter the instruments of their future felicity.

Were it necessary to prove the indescribable advantages furnished by such public granaries, we could find assurance in a small state now forming one of our provinces: Lorraine originally owed an institution of this sort to the kindly forethought of a sovereign who was able to ensure her prosperity for a time. He managed, under sound administration—and with low funds—by reason of profits gained within a short space by this institution, to extend it considerably, thereby enabling the province always to make provision for a few years of scarcity. After the death of Stanislas, the storehouses were destroyed; and Lorraine, like all other provinces, has known the horrors of famine. This public crime, several times suffered in this province, was committed by the intendant then oppressing it, and by the upper tribunal, a party to the outrage; for, through cowardice, they sanctioned its infliction.

Some time after I had laid these two memoranda containing the aforesaid plans in front of M. de Sartine, a Sieur Falconnet—adjutant at the Bastille—did me the honour of coming to talk with me in my cell. He said squarely:

"If M. de Sartine gave you a pension of fifteen hundred francs—*hard cash, yes, hard cash!*—would you drop this project for public granaries?"

My head was full of my notions; and, yet excited by this proposition, I answered promptly, and without reflection, saying:

"I would not renounce the honour of having suggested it, no, not for fifty thousand crowns in cash!"

"Anyhow," the adjutant replied, "if I were you, and in your present state, I should consider myself more than lucky to get such a reward."

"I can understand that," I said, on the instant, playing the little Alexander; "and if I were Falconnet, I too would accept it eagerly."

Immediately he had left me I meditated on the clumsiness of my rejoinders: such blundering might cause trouble; and, to avert this, or to dissipate my fears, I asked to see Father Griffet again, with whom I had had good reason to be satisfied formerly. I told him about this talk, and he agreed with my views. He said:

"You ought to be more wary, in face of the time you have spent in the Bastille. I have no doubt that the officer who came to speak to you was sent by M. de Sartine; and, whatever may have been his motives, your refusal, and especially your manner of announcing it, will prejudice him. I am afraid you may have to repent it."

I have never heard another word on this subject; nor have I heard anything more of the promises made to me by M. de Sartine. Overwhelmed by his silence, I wrote letters and petitions to him; which he never acknowledged. At last, one day, I put the twenty-six letters of the alphabet into an envelope and invited him to show me the method of composing words likely to soften his heart and to make him recall his promises.

It is not surprising that this epistle, like the rest, elicited no reply. Be that as it may, my fate was not changed in the least, nor were the permissions he had granted to me withdrawn. I might promenade on the towers, a favour granted to persons of note alone: ordinary men, *members of the Third Estate*, must keep themselves to the courts, whence there were no views; from the platform, on the contrary, the whole rich basin wherein Paris stands could be seen.

Quite enough accounts have been given concerning the internal regulations at the Bastille, and I shall not repeat them here, having nothing new to tell; but I may at least be permitted to say a word about the food provided: this subject would easily make a chapter in the history of my woes.

The necessity of taking food at the Bastille, and generally in all State prisons, becomes one of the torments of those detained therein. Not that one lacked the wherewithal amply to satisfy these needs; but all things were invariably prepared without care or cleanliness, or, rather, with an affectation certainly showing an indifference most barbarous. The ceaseless monotony with which the same dishes were served, and with a geometric precision so that a prisoner could

have foretold for an entire century what he would have
on Monday, Tuesday, and every day of every week,
seemed yet more repulsive, and in itself enough to
inspire disgust. There was tough butcher's meat,
under-cooked or dried up; vegetables one would have
believed innocent of butter, except for a smell powerful
enough finally and painfully to affect the stomach;
fish sometimes putrid, otherwise quite tasteless; pigs'
trotters scarcely ever worth the trouble of scraping;
or sometimes, and lastly, half-cooked bad pastry,
detestable soup, and wine. This formed the customary
fare in these places, where, nevertheless, the King paid
six, and even ten, livres a day to board each prisoner.
Maybe the governors were ignorant of this odious
regimen, owing to a negligence in supervision; or
perhaps they authorized it from a base cupidity:
certainly they were most cruel to make game of the
prisoners' miseries, to increase and multiply them,
thus poisoning a solitary enjoyment, which otherwise
might have been relished.

I will not insist on these details: doubtless they
contributed much to the making of my captivity
insupportable. However, it was not always possible
for me so to occupy myself, since my years of anguish
were persistently sown with incredible events apparently
succeeding each other, or, rather, accumulating to
lacerate my heart.

One day, as I took my promenade, I spoke with the
sentry on guard who did not know me. He had
served under my father; and he told me that my father
was dead. This fearful blow, for which I was un-
prepared, overpowered me, and I fell unconscious.

I knew how my unhappy father had sought by all
means in his power to appease my oppressors; and
always I lured myself with the hope that sooner or later
they would be touched by his prayers and lamentations.
This resource, perhaps the last remaining to me, was

now removed. Each day a new event occurred to rivet and to reinforce my chains; indeed it seemed as if the whole of nature conspired against me, and that she mustered all her power so to overwhelm me and to drive me to despair.

I have said that the death of my unhappy father robbed me of my last resources; but how can I forget those I found in the inexhaustible tenderness of my mother! At this moment I drench with my tears a host of letters lying before me: only a mother can feel and express herself thus. Her heart was broken, yet she strove to comfort me. She wearied all the ministers with her cries and moans. She wrote to M. Berryer:

"Must I go to my grave without seeing my son again ? my dear son, whom I love so tenderly. Ah! how terribly his sufferings make me suffer! His cruel fate shortens my days and hastens the end."

Hear her when she addresses my persecutress. She wrote to her:

"Madame,
        "My son, having grievously offended you, has groaned for many a long day in the Bastille, and I groan more than he. His sad fate torments me day and night. I feel all the bitterness of his pains, and without having shared his faults. What am I saying ? Alas! I do not even know how he displeased you. He was young at that time, surely led away by others! Ah! how differently he must think to-day! for the thoughts of a captive are unlike the thoughts of a young man in freedom. If he cannot win your forgiveness, Madame, may not I myself win it for him ? Let my fate touch you, have pity on an afflicted mother, be softened by my tears. Death

will soon close my eyes. Do not withhold mercy from my son until I am in my grave. I have only this one child, the solitary hope of my old age. Madame, in your goodness, give him back to me. . . ."

O my mother, you speak of her goodness, abasing yourself even to this extent! Almighty God! A mother's compassion can attain such heights of courage!

" Madame, do not refuse my son to me, the sole consolation of my old age. I pray you graciously to restore him to me in my affliction; yield to my sighs, yield to my tears, yield to my sobs."

And the monster was inflexible.

Many others solicited my deliverance; and my relations and my friends more than once succeeded in interesting this or that of her creatures, or those of M. de Sartine, in my favour; but always they were shocked by these ominous words: " Beware of asking mercy for this wretched knave. You would tremble if you knew his crimes." Thus these foul persecutors, not content with torturing my body, dared to blight and to dishonour me! They carried their inhumanity so far as to alienate my family; they have isolated me on the face of the earth; they have made me an object of opprobrium and of horror to all men. And I was innocent!

My mind, absorbed perpetually by this swarm of cruel thoughts, awoke one day to the light of a hope-ray as it came to illuminate and to console me. I have shown to what extent I could seize the least fancy when it provided a means for breaking my bonds. I saw by a calculation of distances that it would be possible to fling a packet into the Saint-Antoine road from the top of the towers whereon I walked; but from this step

9

to a successful issue was a far stride, for something must be enclosed in the packet; and, once more, I had neither pen, ink, nor paper. Necessity must direct hazard, which could not in itself bring a person into the Saint-Antoine road and facing me at the exact instant when I should throw the packet; a person who would be honest enough to become interested in an unknown miserable creature, pitiful enough to serve me and to give a generous attention, courageous enough to risk the braving of my enemies; and, once more and finally, I must elude the vigilance of my keepers, who never lost sight of me even for a second, having learned to mistrust me. However, as readers have seen, no obstacle ever thwarted me; and I saw no reason now for discouragement.

My first concern was to rid myself of the men who accompanied me on my promenades, ordinarily one Sieur Falconnet, of whom I have previously spoken, and another, a sergeant of the Bastille guard. Falconnet deserved scant consideration; for he was beneath his office, which, in turn, was less than the lowest class in vileness; and a great verbosity served as one of his minor faults. When he accompanied a prisoner he never left him without having told and reiterated all the high facts illustrating his fame. It would be difficult to shake myself from this fellow, and to cure him of his mania for inflicting his panegyrics on me each day. I decided always to contradict him, to deny every fact he advanced, goading him with some sarcasm at each word. This method succeeded, and he never left me save in anger; and eventually he condemned himself to silence when we were together! This was not enough: he must be taught not to follow my movements; and this seemed more difficult. He had his bounden duties, and, since I checked his whim of talking to me, nothing further remained for him except the fulfilment of these duties. Notwithstanding, once again I found a successful method. This consisted in walking with the utmost speed; in effect, I almost ran during my promenades. On the first occasion Falconnet tried to prevent my taking such exercise. I said:

"Don't walk so slowly. I take an airing on my own account, and not on yours. I must sweat, because of my infirmities; and I am trying to make sweat."

He was obliged to leave me alone, and, by degrees, grew accustomed to my behaviour, allowing me to run and to jump as I liked. Meanwhile he could walk at his ease; and, since he could no longer talk to me, he consoled himself with my second keeper, insomuch that very soon their attentions to me were so slight that, when I reached the extremity of the platform opposite to them, they were not at all surprised. Here, occasionally, I stayed for a quarter of an hour, while they, embroiled in conversation, took no notice of me, and did not even think of looking at me.

When this first battery had been dressed, I tried to find someone who would and could hear me, and whose outward aspect alone—since I could not measure him otherwise—would inspire confidence enough to persuade me to deliver the secret of my life to him. From the summit of this platform I could distinguish clearly the various rooms in the houses that surrounded the Bastille, and I took pains to study the folk who occupied these rooms. Primarily, I looked to the women for the execution of my plan, and I wished to find young women; for their affectionate and gentle souls are more susceptible to pity, misfortunes move them with a deeper interest, and their sensibilities are less easily corrupted, giving them a capacity for greater effort. Nature teaches us these truths: I felt, but did not yet know, them. What understanding have I not reached in the sequel! O most truly heroic of women,* how profoundly you have been able to convince me, you who broke my chains, you who—without knowing me, and at the simple tale of my miseries—without friends, protection, fortune, and with no guide other than your heart, crushed my enemies by your virtue, confronted their anger, and overcame your own weaknesses; you with whom my spirit longs ardently to be associated forever, and likewise that the minds of all others shall know your worth! Ah! how my too-slow pen, at the mercy of my impatience, withholds the moment when, by your example, I shall be able to show in what measure the beneficent being, animated by so vital but so rare a sensibility, can recall the august image of Divinity to us on earth!

A fortunate chance helped me even beyond my hopes. I noticed two young women as they worked alone in a room. Their faces seemed pretty and gentle to me; and I was not deceived. One of them glanced in my direction, and I waved to her in a salutation I tried to make seemly and respectful. She drew her sister's attention, who at once looked toward me. Then I saluted the pair, in the same fashion; and they replied with an air of kindliness and interest. From this moment we established a sort of mutual correspondence. Every day I made my visit, and they were equally punctual at our rendezvous. They understood my signs perfectly, and, by their own, let me see in the most expressive manner that they offered willingly to serve me. I showed a packet to them, which they invited me to throw; but I made them understand that the time had not yet arrived, that ere long I should have another to send to them.

---

* Madame Legros, whose conduct toward me equals and perhaps surpasses all that we find most worthy of admiration in the annals of virtue. These details will find their place in the eventual continuation of my Memoirs.

When I returned to my room I occupied myself with the means whereby I could make their goodwill effective. I had not yet fully determined what use I would make of the power of procuring a hearing for myself beyond the walls of my prison. I reflected on this for a while, and was arrested by an idea which, I thought, foreshadowed the single route I must follow.

Any further appeal to intermediaries was no doubt useless; this I had tried too often, and always in vain: my persecutress, in fact, seemed to irritate herself by the efforts I made to appease her; and the tears of my friends, the earnest entreaties of my patrons, had alone, and finally, inflamed her mind and roused her hatred to a greater activity. I could not soothe her: I resolved to make her tremble. From the depths of my prison I would unveil her to the gaze of an indignant France; I would strip her naked in the sight of her lover, who might be terrified by her ugliness. She was on the throne and I in irons; she could dispose of my days, but I could dispose of her honour, or, rather—not to profane this reputable word—I would tear off the mask that served her instead of honour. It would suffice to place the story of her birth and of her shame in sure hands—a story known to me. She, wresting my life from me, had cause to fear my last sigh, which would be terrific! Above all, I should become formidable to her in my grave. For then nothing could arrest the strokes wherewith I meant to make havoc on her. The friends to whose bosom I would entrust my vengeance might warn her of these perils, only leaving her time to forestall them by rendering justice to me. Already I could see her imploring my mercy, and withholding my arm, uplifted to strike. I pictured this haughty woman as she flung herself at my feet, loosened my bonds, bought my silence and her pardon by dint of humiliations;

already I relished the joy of telling her how thoroughly I despised her, and that I scorned to punish her.

I had friends whose zeal was known to me and in whom I felt sure I should find the courage to serve me. First and foremost I proposed to address my memorial to La Beaumelle, well known in the republic of letters by reason of sundry valued works, and because of the hatred of M. de Voltaire.* Charged with such notions, I employed myself in planning this work, which, I confess, I pursued with a mind soaked in the gall that steeped my pen.

However, when I came to the application of this plan, I remembered that I had not procured the things necessary for the writing. Against this obstacle I set the resources which, on all occasions, had served effectively to surmount such obstacles—patience, and a reflectiveness always directed toward the same object; and now, once more, I triumphed, securing my end.

I could not use tablets, needing too many, and the difficulties of hiding them until completion would have been excessive; moreover, unquestionably, they would have broken in the fall from the top of the tower to the pavement. I had books, M. de Sartine having allowed me to buy a few; so I detached the leaves, wrote on the margins and between the lines. I might have taken carp's bones in place of a pen, as formerly; but I had noticed that they would not serve for fine script such as must be written between the lines of a printed work. I used another expedient. I took a

* La Beaumelle was a prisoner at the Bastille in April, 1753, and he remained in the prison for six months. He had had a new edition of Voltaire's *Siècle de Louis XIV* printed, to which he added odes insulting to the House of Orléans. He was again at the Bastille from August, 1756 until August, 1757, on account of his false and scurrilous book, *Notes pour une histoire sur Madame de Maintenon et le siècle dernier.*

According to Funck-Brentano, Latude and D'Alègre found means of corresponding with all the prisoners in the Bastille.—TRANSLATOR'S NOTE.

two-farthing piece, and beat it until it was as flat as
a leaf of paper, and as wide as a crown of six francs;
and this, rolled up, made an excellent point, similar
to those commonly seen in pencils. Now I lacked
nothing save ink; yet I shuddered at reverting to the
cruel method employed hitherto. Apart from the
pain caused by a continued pricking of my fingers
with the buckle-tongue, I had been afraid for some
time lest mortification should set in, and I had reason
to be more fearful of this accident a second time; thus,
yet again, recourse to fresh invention was needful to
attain my object. I could make ink with blacks from
smoke; but how procure this? I had seen neither
light nor fire for eight years; for my enemies, in whom
the most ordinary notion was that I should find means
of escaping from hell, had forbidden, under most
severe penalties, that so much as a pin's head be left
in my hands: hence I was forced to create something
to justify their apprehension.

Firstly, I tried to secure some *amadou* (German
tinder); and to this end, on pretext of a raging tooth-
ache, I begged the sergeant, who was smoking while
in my company on the tower, to lend me his pipe as
a relief, together with something with which to fill and
to light it. He assented. I could neither take his
steel nor the flint; but I filched a scrap of *amadou*.
Once possessed of this little treasure, I was concerned
solely with the means of obtaining fire. I returned
to my room, feigned a sharp colic, and had the surgeon
fetched; who gave me some oil, exactly what I wanted.
I had several earthenware pots, one-time containing
pomade; and in these I set the wick. I made string
with threads drawn from my sheets, took a splat from
my chair and made myself a kind of bow. I attached
my string, leaving this slack enough to fasten a peg,
which I had pointed at one end and rounded at the
other. On one of my walks I had furnished myself

with two pieces of very dry wood, picked up after the recent mounting of a cannon. These I arranged so as to allow for the insertion of the peg. All being thus prepared, I took my two pieces of wood between my knees, held an earthenware pot clasped in my left hand under the rounded extremity of the peg; then I pulled and thrust my bow, and in this way turned the peg, driving it with such speed that very soon it grew hot and ignited the two fragments of wood. I kindled my *amadou* by means of a good supply of lint, already prepared; I blew vigorously, succeeded in procuring a flame, and lighted the lamp.

I could not master my first impulse on seeing this light: I leapt, I danced around, and several minutes were necessary before I could calm my senses and disperse the joyous delirium that agitated me.

Then I placed over the lamp a plate of glazed earthenware, which I had been careful to retain after my last meal; and I used this as a cap for receiving the smoke made by my lamp. I gathered the soot, or blacks, in a piece of paper as fast as it collected in portions; and after a space of six hours I had a very considerable quantity. I tried to pound the black in water, but this proved impossible, since always it floated and I could not dissolve it. I succeeded only by means of a little syrup, obtained by me the next day on the plea of a severe cold; and, thus aided, I made an excellent ink, diluting my smoke-black in a little syrup and water.

Now I had furnished myself with all things necessary; and I wrote the memorial, with the objective mentioned above. I shall give no details here, since they have no further interest. Long ago judgment was passed on this woman by the public; nor can the public hear anything more about her to cause astonishment, nor anything at which it will yet stoop to disgust itself.

I added directions for La Beaumelle to this history of my persecutress; and, in the event of his absence, I addressed the whole to another friend, the Chevalier de Méhégan. The notes, observations, and letters were all in fine condition; and, to conclude, I appended special instructions for my two amiable patronesses, begging them to get in touch with the persons indicated, or, if they could not find them, to substitute others and to interest themselves in obtaining my release. I made a packet of the lot and enclosed it in two skin bags, for which I took the lining from a pair of breeches. I longed for the time to arrive when I might disemburden myself of this heavy load; I was afraid of being searched at any moment; and if these writings were found, I must be lost for ever. I was obliged to exercise great care and cunning; and at last I escaped the danger. During several days I signalled to my two friends to come into the road, there to receive a packet, but they did not appear to understand me; however, on September 21st, 1763, I saw one of them answer the signal, and, taking advantage of the moment when my keepers had their backs to me, I threw the packet with all my strength and cleverly enough to plant it at her feet. I saw her dart forward, seize it, take it to her room promptly; and here her sister awaited her. In less than a quarter of an hour I saw them both go out; and by a most touching gesture they explained to me that they were about to carry the packet to the addresses I had given. I had added to the letter written for them personally that my first duty, my first pleasure, at the instant of deliverance, would be to give them evidence of the feelings inspired in me by their generous conduct. Ah! for nearly thirty years this sacred debt has weighed on my heart. One of the women is dead, but the other lives under conditions far from easy; and only in my heart has she been able to read the expression of my intense gratitude. My infamous persecutors, as a result of their cruelty, have, in a manner, isolated me on this earth; they have delivered me to the torment of living solely on alms-bread; and, to add to my bitter regrets, I am unable to smooth the lot or to beautify the days of those who have lavished so much care on me. My persecutors roll in riches, while I, I . . . Ah! let them at least make it possible for me worthily to repay so many benefits. The sentence about to wither and to condemn them to ignominy is not yet pronounced: I can withhold it. I know I would pardon them at this price.

With what impatience I waited for the moment when I should again see my protectresses! On the following day, as soon as they reappeared, they made many gestures, which in vain I tried to interpret. My most clear perception was that they assumed an air of satisfaction, which, I gathered, no doubt concerned myself alone. They seemed more animated each day, yet I could not satisfy myself. These proceedings lasted for three months and a half, but, so far, I had learned nothing new. Finally, on April 18th, 1764, at a quarter past nine in the morning, I saw them come to the window and unfurl a roll of paper, whereon I read distinctly these words, in large characters:

The Marquise de Pompadour died yesterday, April 17th, 1764.

I thought I saw the heavens open. The idea that there could be one day's delay in the breaking of my bonds did not even enter my head: never had I committed a fault that demanded legal vengeance, for my sole crime had been to excite the anger of this imperious woman; and she was dead. Could this sentiment possibly outlive her? Invariably M. Berryer had said— and all who sought to comfort me had incessantly repeated—that her disgrace or death would make end to my miseries. In the certainty of this statement, I packed my trunk; for at any moment I expected the arrival of someone who would announce the order for my release. What was my amazement when several days passed without my hearing a single word on the subject! I wrote at once to M. de Sartine. I reminded him that since I was not guilty, nor had I known either accuser or judge, I could only have been kept at the Bastille by the orders of the Marquise de Pompadour, and that her death must mean the end of my captivity, likewise of her vengeance.

The officers of the Bastille, the turnkeys, and, in general, all who were attached to the place, had received the most explicit command to say nothing whatsoever to the prisoners about the death of the Marquise. Picture the astonishment of the lieutenant of police when he read my letter! He came immediately, in haste, and had me brought before him; and, with every sign of anger, he asked whence I had received this news. His question, and especially the tone of his demand, taught me that in all probability I should endanger those who had apprised me if I were faint-hearted enough to mention them. I told M. de Sartine that, since he seemed to attach so great an importance to such a trifle, I could not fail to recognize his motive; also that he—too acute not to perceive the results of the avowal he demanded—could disembowel me before I would give up the secret.

He insisted, and carried his meanness to the extent of saying:

" Answer me! That is the price of your freedom."

I could not master a frenzy of indignation. I said to him:

" I seem to see Mahomet II as he takes twelve serving-boys and has them ripped open so that he may know which of them has eaten five of his figs."

He stammered and flushed, and went off after promising to do what he could for me.

I allowed a few days to pass; then, hearing no further

news, I wrote to him. I overwhelmed him with petitions and remonstrances; for, unable to soften him, at least I wanted to wear him down by my importunities. He sent word that *he had not forgotten me, and was working for me efficaciously.* The officer who brought this message emphatically stressed the word *efficaciously.* He, on several occasions, had witnessed the promises M. de Sartine had made to secure the just reward I could claim for services rendered. Forthwith I grasped my pen. I informed M. de Sartine that if I must purchase the certainty of reward by some further days of captivity, I would make a formal renouncement thereof; and that if I were to have a hundred thousand crowns at the end of six months, I should pay too dearly for them by spending this additional time in the Bastille: that the solitary favour I beseeched was the justice due to me on so many counts; that I renounced everything, forgave everything, provided that my freedom should be granted to me instantly.

I heard nothing more from him. How slow the drag of days under such circumstances! What more dreadful plight than when the mind, caught in a labyrinth, oppressed alternately by impatience and cruelty, hope and despair, turns unceasingly on itself! The officers of the Bastille seemed indignant, and felt some pity—perhaps for the first time. One of them let me suspect that the heirs of the Marquise, fearing the too just claims of the numerous victims of her hatred, had no doubt bought the silence of the ministers on whose power the stifling of their last sighs might yet depend. This reflection reminded me of the precise orders given to all who came in contact with the prisoners at the Bastille, whereby they must not mention this woman's death; also of M. de Sartine's fury when he heard that I knew of it, and of his threats, intended to extract my secret—and of his entire conduct, certainly peculiar, and maintained to such an end. These observations and calculations eventually led me astray, for I believed I was lost beyond recall. I imagined a new conspiracy more terrible than the first: I had been the victim of an angry woman's tyranny; now I might become the victim of a minister's baseness, more severe and, therefore, more vile. The one might weaken or wither; the other, more deliberate, might be eternal.

My spirit was occupied with and embittered by these thoughts, and I took counsel alone with the frenzy possessing me. I unbosomed my soul, and my rage, on paper, and in a paroxysm I sent the writing thus inspired to M. de Sartine. I was powerless to shame the man, but anyhow, I would force him to come and strangle me, so ending my anguish. This new crime, however, demanded some kind of energy, and his spirit was incapable of such a thing.

I can hear all would-be sensible men, subsequent to this statement, blaming me harshly and maybe finding a justification in the like conduct for the atrocious cruelties afflicting me so long; or, generous, they may marshal their so-called sensibilities, and excuse me in compassion. Ah! let these cold reasoners learn rather to pity the unhappy wretch devoured by a fervid susceptibility; let them learn to know what a welter of sighs provoked by despair can bring forth. Above all, let them learn that he who respectfully kisses the oppressing tyrant's hand is but a coward, not worthy of pity, and that Socrates perhaps appears so great to us only because he dared to defy Anitus.

I sent this letter on July the 27th, 1764. A generous tyrant—and a tyrant may be generous on occasion— would have been moved by the reading; he would have been shamed, and might have pardoned. M. de Sartine had me thrown into a dungeon: that was his answer, and one worthy of him.

There I remained on bread and water until the following 14th of August. Probably he reflected that the Bastille officers, having witnessed his former promises to me and his previous conduct, easily divined his motives; and like all despots—who, even as they crush us by their vices, dare try to feign virtue—he allowed a rumour to spread throughout the prison suggesting his inclination to set me free, but, since he must accustom me gradually to breathing in a new atmosphere, he was about to transfer me for a few months to a convent of monks. Consequently, I was taken from my dungeon during the night of the 14th to 15th of August, 1764; and, loaded with irons of all sorts, and under the escort of a police-officer named Rouillé, assisted by two bailiff's men, I was carried to a hackney-coach. There a scene ensued perhaps more outrageous than anything hitherto recorded to make one cringe; for the cruelty was more cold-blooded, and therefore more revolting.

My keepers attached an iron chain to my neck, passing the end under the fold of my knees: one placed a hand over my mouth and his other hand behind my head; meanwhile his companion pulled the afore-mentioned chain sharply; hence, actually, they doubled me in two. The pain I felt was so excruciating, I thought my loins were broken; and I am sure that such a pain at least equalled the experience of miserable fellows dying on the wheel. In this state I was taken from the Bastille to Vincennes. M. de Sartine must have been satisfied to hear that the executioners had carried out his commands so faithfully. In order to enhance his joy, he had a statement made of the full details. I have in my hands the report of the police-officer Rouillé, who gave the facts. However, we have not yet reached the end: we pass from horror to horror; and I give warning that I am about to reveal things fit to terrify the imagination of a tyrant.

The lieutenant of police, subsequent to the letter I wrote to him on July 27th, had sworn to ruin me.

My death would not have satisfied his vengeance:
to gratify that he muſt torture me, glutting himself
with my pangs; but, to this end, I muſt be isolated, and
to a degree impossible even at the Baſtille; nor had he
the right to transfer me elsewhere, since M. de Saint-
Florentin, Miniſter of Paris at that time, could alone
give such an order. Here is the memorandum addressed to him by M. de Sartine for this purpose, one
found in the Baſtille on July 16th laſt, by a certain
Sieur Boileau and a Sieur Rousselin, tax-clerks, who
handed it to me. No doubt a God—the God avenging
crimes—preserved this document for service on a
future day, so to confound, and to teach us to know,
this loathsome miniſter.

Before giving the memorandum, I muſt mention that
I lay in the Baſtille under the name of Daury: in this
place it was the cuſtom thus to baptize, on their entrance,
those of the prisoners who might have powerful patrons,
since, to anyone soliciting their release, answer could
be made that among the Baſtille prisoners no one
bearing the name given was known. This is not the
moment to make reflections on such a subject; my indignation spurs me onward. Now hear M. de Sartine.

OBSERVATIONS
On Some Passages of these Memoranda

His ferocity! . . . My friends,
my many and respectable patrons,
answer for me here, saying if ever
you have found me malicious and

MEMORANDUM*
Presented by M. de Sartine to M. de Saint-Florentin

" The longer Daury remains
a prisoner, the more his
ferocity and malice increase."

---

* This memorandum, in the writing of the Sieur Duval, firſt clerk
at this period (1764), has a poſtscript in M. de Sartine's hand; by whom
these words are written in the margin: "Valid for orders. Inform
M. Guyonnet that he is to be put in the dungeons."

I possess other letters from these two persons: anyone may come
to my house and compare the handwritings.

ferocious.! How often, pitying me
for all the ill I have suffered, have you
not applauded the gentleness of my
character ? Doubtless my intelligence has not the vivacity, the amiable
delicacy, which knowledge of the
world alone can give, and which one
acquires with difficulty in prisons ; but
my cowardly persecutor accuses my
heart, and you have always found this
loving and sensitive : could it have
changed if for a moment it had ever
been *ferocious?* I shall give in their
place two letters from the governor of
Vincennes testifying to my natural
gentleness and absolute resignation—
and testifying to M. de Sartine. . . .

This may be judged in accord with
the way I behaved myself each time
I regained my liberty. It will be seen
presently what use I made of this,
especially in relation to M. de Sartine,
when I was fortunate enough to screen
myself from his anger for a little
time.

"He declares that he is
capable of resort to the worst
of crimes, and of committing
an evil act, if he is set free."

And what difference did his saying
this make to me then ? I had been a
prisoner for seventeen years. During
that period false news of the sort had
been repeated to me perhaps a thousand times ; ought I to have put more
faith in this now, because M. de Sartine sent to announce it. . . . *The
time for my liberation was not yet
determined.* And why not ? Who prevented this ? What was my crime ?
Where were my accusers, and the
judgment that condemned me to
suffer a continual and an ever renewed
torture for seventeen years ?

"Since July 1st and August
13th last, when I sent to tell
him to be patient, and that
the time for his liberation,
approaching, was not yet determined, there is no kind of
excess, coarseness, insult, and
threat he has not used to
make himself formidable."

I had become a scoundrel in prison !
Then I was not a scoundrel when I
went thither ? Clumsy tyrant ! you

"The memory of Madame
la Marquise is a horror and a
scourge to him : he lavishes

did not see that you betrayed yourself: you did not conceive that if I had in truth become a scoundrel in prison, it was you who kept me there unjustly; that your barbarity goaded my despair; that you must take the guilt of my crimes, which would recoil on your own head! You trampled every law under foot, but you could not defy divine justice; and it is you she ought to have punished.

Was not this my crime? Was not this the moment when I became a scoundrel? . . . Until then, M. de Sartine had promised my freedom to me; until then he had praised me, approving my various plans relative to public affairs, offering to ensure my reward some day; until then he had granted me the favour, rare in the Bastille, of promenading on the towers. If before writing this letter I had been a *scoundrel*, a *ferocious* man, would he have behaved thus? Or, if I was such at this time as he has dared to picture, why has he not since continued the same conduct?

WITH HUMANITY! . . .
And he had me put in the dungeons on straw, with bread and water.

All this is merely an imposture: it was the day after he received the fatal letter that he had me put in the dungeons; from that moment nothing was said to me; I neither wrote, nor could write, anything.

In irons, flung on straw, in a dungeon, I interfered with the service

the most scoundrelly epithets on her, *because he has himself become a scoundrel in his prison.* If she had lived, he says he would have wrought a catastrophe (p. 7 of his letter, July 27th). The King himself is not safe from his frenzies and insolent railleries."

"After the letter of July 27th, wherein he uttered the most atrocious insults and serious threats against me, I behaved with *humanity* toward him."

"I disdained his frenzies and sent assurances to him by the major, to whom I had written that his prison term would be shortened. He replied with such insolent letters that I had him put in the dungeons, of which he makes derision."

"This man, who is more enterprising than words can

10

of the Bastille ! But it was necessary to make foundation for what follows in the memorandum. I shudder. Let us finish. tell, interferes considerably with the service of the Bastille."

AND THERE TO FORGET HIM ! . . . "It would be a suitable moment to transfer him to the Donjon of Vincennes, where there are fewer prisoners than in the Bastille, *and there to forget him.*"

"If M. le Comte de Saint-Florentin approves of this procedure, he is respectfully requested to send the orders necessary to this effect."

And there to forget him ! . . . Did ever code of despotism contain atrocities like this ? And if the genius of evil, invoked by pagans, had dictated orders, would they have been otherwise expressed ? And could he have aped this calm, cold-blooded cruelty ? Ah ! no doubt this man, to be capable of a like crime, must have quelled all natural feeling in his heart ! Did the knave therefore, and also, believe he could stifle his remorse ?

In consequence of the order so urgently solicited, and signed by Saint-Florentin, I was put in a dungeon the moment I reached Vincennes. Once again I became ill: my physical and moral faculties grew weaker each day. The governor, M. Guyonnet at this time, took pity on me. He was an upright, virtuous man, who kept the position so ill-suited to him for too little a time, his unworthy successor having caused the prisoners deeply to regret M. Guyonnet and his benefactions.

I have seen this good and estimable man shed tears at the story of my wrongs; and he was intrepid enough to soothe them and to take me from my dungeon. He had a comfortable room assigned to me, where sometimes he came; and he shared my indignations against the barbarity of my enemy. In addition, he secured for me a promenade of two hours each day in the gardens of the Château.

The most precious factor in this privilege was the hope that sooner or later it would provide the means to yet another escape. During eight successive months I benefited by this exercise, without discovering any facilities for escape. I was so closely watched over that it seemed impossible to carry out any plan, and in the solitude of my prison I could scarcely conceive or dwell on any idea, even momentarily; for my keepers, warned of all I might devise to recover freedom, seemed to read into my soul, and they fettered my thought. Accordingly I could only leave the task of regaining my liberty to some unforeseen hazard whereby I might have the courage, and enough presence of mind, to profit. Such a chance occurred, and one I was indeed far from anticipating.

On November 23rd, 1765, I made my promenade about four o'clock in the afternoon, the weather being fairly serene; but, on a sudden, a dense mist arose; and immediately the idea flashed into my mind that it might favour my flight. This notion arrested me, enthralled me; but how deliver myself from my keepers, excluding the several sentries who blocked all passages? I had two keepers and a sergeant with me, nor did they leave me for a second. I could not fight them: their arms, number, physical force, gave them the advantage over me. I could not slip away furtively and outdistance them; for it was their business to accompany me, and to follow all my movements. A necessary bold stroke might allow me to dart from them while they were gazing around and striving to collect their wits. I spoke brazenly to the sergeant, calling his attention to the thick mist, risen so rapidly. I said to him:

" What think you of the weather?"

" Very bad, sir," he answered.

"And I—I find it excellent for escape," I said at once with the utmost calm and simplicity.

As I uttered these words I used my elbows, scattering the two sentries to the right and to the left of me. I gave the sergeant a violent shove, and fled. I continued within close hail of a third sentry, who did not notice me until I had passed on. Then they joined one with the other, crying out here and there:

"Stop! Stop!"

Now the guards assembled. Windows were opened, everybody ran; everybody shouted, repeating:

"Stop! Stop!"

I could not escape.

Promptly I conceived the notion of profiting by my circumstance, so to make my way through the crowd that prepared to arrest me. I too shouted, and more loudly than they:

"Stop! Stop!"

I made a gesture with my hand, illustrating this demand; and they, deceived by the trick, and by the accommodating mist, imitated me, running with me in pursuit of the fugitive, at whom I seemed to point. I outdistanced them, and had but one more step to take, being already at the far end of the royal court. Yet another sentry remained, however, one difficult to cozen; for, naturally, he would suspect, and in duty must arrest, the first man appearing before him. My calculations were only too just. The sentry, on hearing the first shouts, had taken position in the middle of a path very narrow at this point; and, to add to misfortune, this sentry, one Chenu, knew me. I reached him. He barred the way, calling on me to stop or he would ram his bayonet into me.

"My good Chenu," I said, "you dare not. Your instructions are to stop me, and not to kill me."

I had reduced my pace, approaching him slowly; and, near to him, I sprang at his musket, snatched it from his hands, and with such force that the unforeseen movement knocked him down. I leaped over his body, threw the musket ten paces from him, in fear that he might fire on me—and once more I was free.

I hid myself without difficulty in the park. I avoided the high-road, jumped over the wall, and waited until night before entering Paris. I did not hesitate to go to the two young women with whom I had made acquaintance from the height of the Baſtille towers, and who, apparently, had served me with so much zeal; and ere long they proved to me that such zeal had arisen from the heart, and that I had, in faɕt, inspired them with a moſt urgent and tender intereſt. They recognized me at once and received me with affeɕtion, having believed I muſt be dead; for they could not imagine my delaying to send news of myself to them, had I been free. I learned that they were named Lebrun, their father being a wig-maker. Death has taken one of them since that time; and a brother inhabits the same eſtablishment at this moment, where he has a perfumery business. I asked them for details about the use they had made of the packet and papers thrown by me from the summit of the Baſtille towers. They said they had followed my inſtruɕtions; and, as I soon perceived, they had followed them with more zeal than intelligence. My demands were direɕted to MM. de la Beaumelle, de la Condamine, and the Chevalier de Méhégan. The two firſt named were not in France, and the other had been married recently; and his wife, hearing that a packet brought to him came from the Baſtille, had sought to prevent even his acceptance of it, for she knew that the more innocent the unhappy wretch whose plaints were contained therein, the greater the danger of defending him. The Lebrun young ladies were unable to find patrons for me, and depended on themselves alone; but their hearts, though indeed faithful, were not greatly enlightened. Furthermore, the Marquise died while they were prosecuting their designs; and they, having heard no news from me in the sequel, ceased to occupy themselves with my affairs. Nevertheless, their welcome proved that they had not failed to think of me, or to feel interest in me. They had been most cautious in refraining from speaking of me and of all they were doing for me to their father; for his prudence might have led him to oppose their efforts in fear of consequences to his family. They made me acquainted with him, gave some of his linen to me, also a room, and fifteen livres from their own pockets; and at meal-times they brought food to me: in short, they lavished their care and attentions on me, and with an alacrity that showed the goodness and compassion of their hearts. What sentiment could animate them other than delight in doing good?

Immediately I had recovered from my first emotions, and when tranquillity and a little rest had restored a mastery of mind and spirit, I engaged myself with the means of recovering my freedom and of escaping from this new captivity. I shall astonish my readers, and perchance embitter them against myself, by the story of my conduct at this pass. When I say that I wrote to M. de Sartine they will cry out at my extravagance and refuse to sympathize further with the misfortunes I was about to call down on myself. I have need of their esteem, their pity, and I must justify myself in their view: let them but deign to follow me for a moment in an account of the reflections that directed me.

M. de Sartine had overpowered me with the most odious persecutions; he had judged me by his own standard, and, therefore, naturally, he believed I must be his enemy. Probably he did me the honour of being afraid of me; whereas I, far from resembling him, had more need of rest than of vengeance. I was incapable of pretence, and I could not speak to him

of respect; but, since he was minister, I owed submission to him, and, the State being despotic, I must
accordingly be his subject. I sought to disarm his
hate, otherwise it would pursue me everywhere; for
only too well I had learned that no place existed where
I could defy him and shelter myself from his attacks!
And, had there been such a place, how could I reach it,
how leave the kingdom and, above all, Paris? Everyone vaunted the indefatigable activity of M. de Sartine:
he knew everything, he saw everything, was informed
of all things, and no one has been able further to carry
the art, so famous in France, of *policing*, of maintaining
order and of doing well by force of baseness. Could
I believe his vigilance would be less effective when
an indulgence of his passion was at stake than when
his concerns were with outside interests? Infallibly
I should have been discovered in flight, likewise in
my retreat.

Consequently, I wrote to him, urging him to forget
my insults dictated by a delirium of mind; I assured
him of silence and an absolute submission, and, to
convince him that my repentance must be genuine, I
besought him to become my patron, thus acquiring
rights over the gratitude which forthwith would
supplant all other sentiments in my heart. I wrote to
him:

" You have approved and praised my military plan;
the King has adopted it, reinforcing our armies by more
than twenty thousand excellent fusiliers. Stoop to
recall how you yourself, in presence of the officers of
the Bastille, promised to secure a reward for me.
To-day I could address myself to the Duke de Choiseul
and demand this from him as an act of justice; but I
prefer to await it as a favour from you."

I begged him, if he adopted my ideas, to have black
crosses marked on a door of the Tuileries, and in yet
another place indicated by me. On seeing these signs

I would furnish him with the means of sending a written paper to me, in which he could give assurance that I should enjoy peacefully the liberty I had won for myself, and that he would interest himself, as he had promised to do, in obtaining the rewards which, though due to me on so many counts, I meant to claim only on one count. I gave my word of honour that, on the instant, I would come, bringing all my papers, promising obedience.

At an early hour on the morrow I sent some trustworthy folk to see if the signals were displayed. They saw nothing. I have heard since, yet too late, that the police-officers charged with the business of making the crosses I asked for, were sent; but, instead of making these marks on the door-timbers, they put them on paper attached to these same doors, and which passersby tore down ere the arrival of my emissaries: however, had they found them, I should have been no further advanced. Beware of suspecting for a moment that M. de Sartine had consulted his sense of honour or of delicacy; for his promptitude in answering my demand, as will be seen presently, was only a trap, another scurvy deed.

I fancied I had nothing save wrath and tyranny to expect from him, and I sought other means of escaping him. M. the Prince de Conti had formerly honoured me with certain interest and had promised his protection. I went to him, flung myself at his feet; and he condescended to welcome me, receiving me with the agreeable mildness peculiar to him; which, had he but followed the dictates of his heart, might have earned for him the permanent love of his fellow-citizens. I told the story of my wrongs to him: he was revolted by so many horrors, and, after allowing me to talk with him for full three hours, gave orders that some relief should be afforded to me, and promised to send his secretary to speak with M. de Sartine.

This secretary told me he would come to my dwelling after his interview with the lieutenant of police, whom he meant to see that day. The interview in fact took place; but the magistrate damped the secretary's ardour, and persuaded him artfully and by infamous calumny that I had imposed on the Prince and was unworthy of his kindness. This too credulous man, seeing in M. de Sartine merely a public functionary who reported facts and had no personal enmities to avenge, blindly accepted all these imputations and easily misled the Prince. Such are the great! Only too often their hearts may be tender, susceptible to pity, yet rarely have they energy enough to search out and to recognize timid innocence: they know how to help innocence, on occasion, but never how to avenge it.

The lieutenant of police, thus warned of the course I was pursuing, forestalled all my efforts: knowing my patrons, he saw them, and prejudiced them against me; and when, later, I presented myself, all doors were shut against me. I sank into despair; and the Chevalier de Méhégan, my friend of whom I have spoken already, came to add to my despair by telling me how M. de Sartine and the Marquise de Pompadour's brother were intriguing against me on all sides; how I was being sought throughout Paris; and that my description had been sent to all the mounted police, and a reward of one thousand crowns had been offered to anyone who might arrest me.

The cowards! Such are the arms with which they attacked me! They feared lest my sighs should be heard; they feared that I might find a refuge whence I could denounce them to the vengeance of the law. Alas! and this sanctuary, too, would have been closed to me.* However, another tribunal remained before

* Subsequently, and under less critical conditions, one of my most zealous patrons, M. de Comeyras, an advocate defending me at that time, had prepared a memorial to be made public and which he

which they would tremble to find themselves arraigned:
how could they defy public opinion, that inflexible
judge dreaded by despots, and which even they are
compelled to respect! M. de Sartine dared to claim
the title of an upright man, even of a virtuous man;
and no doubt he was afraid that a venturesome hand
might rip from him the deceptive mask with which
he arrayed himself so artfully: this was the motive
force of his entire behaviour toward me.

I could discover but one expedient, which seemed
exceedingly perilous as a means; yet, since it might be
the last remaining to me, I must try it. Everybody
praised the noble and frank loyalty of the Duke de
Choiseul, minister at that time. He was raised too
high above men by his talents and genius to be other
than absolute; yet, too great to be a despot, he knew
how to respect unhappy men; anyhow, public opinion
painted him thus for the general gaze, and I trusted
in the portrait. I wrote to him, full of confidence.
He was with the Court at Fontainebleau. I begged
from him a moment's audience on December 18th,
the day when I expected to reach Fontainebleau,
urging him to be my judge; and, as a sole favour, I
asked him not to pronounce on my fate until he had
heard me.

I set out on the 15th. Can I possibly recall the
events of this journey, and all the horror of my position!
I was forewarned that M. de Sartine, wishful at any
price to make sure of my person, had instigated a strict

---

expected would produce a lively impression in my favour. In taking
this step he had alone consulted his customary guide, an honest and
sympathetic mind inspiring his spirit to great activity. He was told
that advocates of the Paris Parlement could not prepare memorials
for those who were under *lettres-de-cachet*, and therefore the plates
must be destroyed. This is a fact for reflection ; and it is chiefly to be
observed that the order of advocates subjected to this rule was perhaps
the body who had dared to act and to speak with the greatest measure
of freedom under the *ancien régime*. . . .

search for me. I conceived readily the outstanding
importance to him of closing Court avenues against
me, nor did I doubt that I was especially marked down,
and should be looked for on the road to Fontainebleau;
accordingly I could not take one step without fear of
discovery. The exactitude of my calculations will
be seen presently. Always I kept far from the high-
road and walked only at night, so to avoid the many
dangers. The cold was intense, the ground covered
with snow and ice. I fell into ditches, since I lacked
the strength to leap over them; I tore my clothes as I
passed through hedges; I had no money: moreover, I
shunned all sight and could not address myself to anyone. I had nothing but a fragment of bread for
provision, my solitary nourishment. I hid myself in a
field throughout the day of the 16th; and, after walking
for two nights, I arrived at Fontainebleau on the
morning of the 17th, exhausted by pain, hunger,
fatigue and despair. In this state I presented myself
at the Duke de Choiseul's audience. He was told of
my presence in his antechamber, and gave instructions
that I must wait for a while. Some minutes later I
saw him pass; and he took seat in his chair and was
carried to the Duke de la Vrillière's house. I did
not then know the hatred and great fear inspired by
this mere name. Were these two ministers holding
council to ruin me? Were they concerned with me, or
did the satellites of the lieutenant of police profit by
this momentary absence of the Duke de Choiseul to
execute orders so imperiously issued to them? I
have never yet been able to penetrate into this frightful
maze.* Be that as it may, shortly afterward, two

* The Sieur de Latude always believed that the Duke de Choiseul
was the accomplice, on this occasion, of the cowardly lieutenant of
police, to whom the Duke had delivered him ; but Latude had no proofs.
The historian of these memoirs is far from accepting such notions.
Author of a eulogy on the Duke de Choiseul, and adopted by an Academy,

police-officers, Fleury and Levasseur, of whom the last, I believe, is yet alive, came to tell me that the Dukes de Choiseul and de la Vrillière wished to speak to me; and they had received orders to take me to the house of the latter. I followed them. They placed me in a chair at the door and set off with me; but, instead of taking me, as they had said, to the minister, they took me to a place which seemed to be the Town Hall, where they kept me within sight in a room until another emissary came to announce that the orders were that I must be taken back to Paris and put in the Conciergerie under guard of the tribunals, who would render the justice owing to me and would pronounce on my fate.

I had become inured to this contemptible form adopted by all the tools of the police, and this time I was not duped by their lies. I should have believed myself only too happy in being subjected to legal supervision and admitted to the presence of the tribunals, where, after a hearing, I should have been judged. I knew my enemies dreaded this as much as I desired it. I saw clearly that I was lost. I had exposed M. de Sartine to shame; I had ventured to wound his self-love and to defy his authority. What might I not have to fear now? I was accustomed to no judges other than my tormentors; and this time hatred would inspire them.

It is difficult to imagine how I was able to listen at that time, and to recall the conversation between the police-officers and myself during the journey. How

he studied for a considerable time and believes he has seized the character of this minister, in which all things, even the faults, have the imprint of a great mind. A man such as he might make brilliant mistakes, but never vile or idle ones; the behaviour accredited to him by the Sieur de Latude could have been worthy of M. de Sartine alone. The interpretation given by the writer of this note to the fact in question is more natural, more likely, and probably more true.—NOTE BY THIERRY.

did my oppressed mind find strength enough to gather all they told to me of the motives and morality of my persecutors ? They expressed keen surprise at having discovered me at Fontainebleau. All roads leading thither, they said—also the Château avenues, the gates to the town, the barges—were so closely guarded by men posted to arrest me that I must have made myself invisible, thus to get as far as the Duke de Choiseul's. I then learned that no crime was comparable to that of daring to complain to a minister, none so severely punished. These police-officers cited the provincial deputies sent recently to the King to denounce the exactions of several Intendants, and punished as dangerous and seditious persons. Everyone connected with the administration, all the agents, all members of the redoubtable body which this host of despots had the effrontery to call the *Government*, demanded altars and a creed; yet, like the malign gods of paganism, to whom incense was offered solely to mitigate their wrath, these modern *Arimanes*, careless of our veneration and of our homage, inspired fear alone and laid claim to nothing but our obedience.

The too short hours of my joyless freedom had run out, and my dream was in ruin. On awakening, I recognized the towers and the Donjon of Vincennes.

LINGUET

INTRODUCTION

L INGUET says of himself, in a minor work among a multitude now almost forgotten, that, although he wanted to be peaceable and could be indulgent, he was vindictive by Reason; and, one might add, since invariably he at least strove to be reasonable, frequently he appears to have been vindictive. He, like Latude, was a notorious product of his time; and, unlike Latude, he spent most of his amazingly crowded life outside prison rather than in it, and, therefore, made great impress on his time: Voltaire named him the Parisian Rousseau. There was something of Rousseau, much of Voltaire, more of his own egregious self in Linguet, together with sundry unamiable traits, also a disposition to regard himself as a hero; whereby, once more, he squares with Latude. His portrait shows the profile of a keen, incisive man, more powerful than pleasing, with the brow of a thinker, the nose of a ferrety lawyer, the chin of a heavy-weight champion; and there is the so-called Mephistophelian lift of sparse eyebrows, a cynical yet not essentially cruel curl to the lips: a little atrabilious fellow, his nerves seemingly strung to the top of the compass, his muscles and sinews strained, as if outward and inward composure were unknown to him; and his life and his works prove indubitably that, as a rule and in effect, he was no more composed than a live volcano.

One of his outstanding claims to position in history rests on his being the originator of political journalism, which, presumably, earns him laurels; and he was a publicist who repeatedly and thoroughly scared his enemies and alarmed his friends. He inaugurated a new form of polemical oratory, he posed as the first advocate of his day, until his immense prowess and his ineradicable habit of mind and expression incited hatred, jealousy, dread, and led to his being struck off the rolls; and he figures in this book as a prisoner in, and an indirect demolisher of, the Bastille. He might well have taken for his life-text: Woe to them that are at ease in Zion. He could rage with the fury of a Hebrew prophet, and on occasion scold like a verbose fish-wife, against what seemed to him the folly or the knavery that stalked earth to cajole men into a mean submission or torment them to extinction.

If Linguet had been endowed with philosophic calm and a gift of ripe, rich humour; if he had controlled his rampant zeal with a work-a-day notion of fitness, sweetened his imagination with benevolence, and tempered his inflexible, narrow logic with common sense, he might have been notable among seers of the world: but he was prone to destroy in anger, slow to construct in measure. Such a man has a prodigious faculty for creating enemies, only a slight aptitude for acquiring and retaining affectionate disciples: and there stands Linguet.

Generally he remained bondslave to his own critical views, though they were surprisingly kaleidoscopic; and his imprudence seems to have been considerable. He made a god, or a jest, of Authority, in accord with the notion of the moment; and, in his devious and noisy quick-march to the grave, turn by turn he became the helpmate of the philosophers, and the apparent enemy. He defended the Jesuits, then denounced the monks; wrote for religion, and sometimes derided it; insulted the great, and flattered them; scoffed at democracy, then fought for it; railed at tyranny, and advocated despotism; and so on and on to the end of

PLATE V

SIMON NICOLAS HENRI LINGUET

[face p. 162

the ſtormy chapter. In short, he had the dialeſtical mind, yearned for perfeſtion, and discovered flaws in all creatures and inſtitutions.

He figures as a paragon, a rascal, and a number of other things contradiſtory and extreme in countless memoirs, chronicles, and pamphlets of his day; accordingly his biographers in books and essays have either accused him of moſt sins in and out of the decalogue, have imposed several of the beatitudes on him, or have been puzzled and ambiguous—which is not surprising. Funck-Brentano, Bournon, and others of the school, dislike him, either mildly or intemperately; Monselet, in his *Les oubliés et les dédaignés* (new edition, Paris, 1876), gives him firſt place and seeks to do honour to him; Monin, in his edition of the *Mémoires* (Paris, 1889), is obviously suspicious of him; and the moſt fulsome and perhaps the beſt account of him comes from Jean Cruppi (*Un avocat journaliſte au 18ᵉ sicèle*, Paris, 1895), and affords a vivid piſture of the Parlement and the Bar in Linguet's dynamic time. Even a Cruppi, however, after referring to his subjeſt's vaſt talent, declares that the man, in revolt againſt the ideas of his period, was reduced to a sort of Captain Fracasse by his foibles.

Linguet was born at Rheims on the 14th of July, 1736, exaſtly fifty-three years before the ſtorming and fall of the Baſtille, sired by an earneſt, intrepid humaniſt, who, after professorial work at the College of Navarre, Paris, and a dabbling in Jansenism, visions, magic, was sent thence, exiled to Champagne. Thus Linguet was "born under the auspices of a *lettre-de-cachet*," as he wrote, and reiterated. In his youth, and after the death of his parents, he went to the Navarre College, there welcomed in memory of his "martyred father"; and he showed unusual ability as a scholar, advanced rapidly, especially in Latin, and took the three firſt University prizes. Linguet, however, hampered by poverty, had to renounce an already coveted academic career, becoming secretary to the Duke de Deux-Ponts, the future sovereign of the Palatinate; with whom he travelled widely and happily, until, falsely accused of theft, he loſt his temper and chided the Duke; which, so to speak, is the firſt hiſtoric inſtance of the militant habit developed by Linguet into something like mania, finally disaſtrous to him. On several occasions in his manhood he was charged with thefts and cheateries, and always ridiculously, though his innumerable enemies, grubbing and scraping in the paſt for filth to throw, used such fictions adroitly. Later, when the Order of Advocates enumerated the griefs provoked by their culprit, they wrote: "You abused the confidence of the Duke when you were attaché to him . . . "; and there are slanderous examples of the sort sown heavily in writings againſt Linguet.

He left the service of the Duke, and in high dudgeon, susceptible to insult and inclined by temperament to brood over such things; and he joined forces with Dorat, one as ambitious and as impoverished as himself. They took a grimy lodging in Paris and tried to get bread, and fame, as men of letters, Linguet having commenced with poetry and tragedy, works now utterly ignored, and despised then; and, failing lamentably and bitterly, he loſt his earlier though sporadic complaisance, quarrelled with Dorat, left him. In Linguet's twenty-sixth year the Jesuits were expelled from France by the Parlement. About the same time Rousseau's *Emile*, also his *Contrat social*, appeared, and added to the wrack of conflicting opinions exercising all intelligent, and many unintelligent, men during those pregnant and prophetic years. As Cruppi says, it was necessary to take sides either with the Philosophers, the Jesuits, or the Parlement. Linguet, by inſtinct, and doubtless with some perversity, chose the more perilous line of action and thought; and, influenced by a friendly Jesuit, he declared himself for reaction, wrote and printed bad verses, together with stinging, lurid prose, on behalf of the banished.

Forthwith he attracted attention, and supplemented disfavour by publishing his *Histoire de l'âge d'Alexandre*, a ponderous, ill-digested affair, sooty in phrase, bombastic, though it starts modestly enough with a statement of Linguet's tentative claims in Letters, preliminary to the argument that Alexander, Cæsar, and the like heroes of antiquity, were more fatal in their wars and policies to humanity than the Neros and Domitians in their " tranquil and reflective cruelty "; that historians praise Cæsar for having slaughtered a million men in his campaigns; and that a Caligula, a Commodus, appear to Linguet in the comparison as prodigies of gentleness and clemency. Pedants and others swinged Linguet for these declarations, whereupon he set up a permanent opposition-tent; nor did he ever leave it for more than a short vacation, his eclectic delight in attack being irremediable and unbridled.

Linguet forsook Paris again, certainly not because the place might become too sultry for him, since nothing could be too sultry for a Linguet, but owing rather to an ominous shortage of cash; and he allied himself to the Prince de Beauvau and went with the troops to Spain. He soon had a surfeit of tepid campaigning, left the Prince, wandered aimlessly over Europe, thought of taking to industry in Lyons and of exploiting an invention for making soap! This innocuous sally quickly repelled him as a prospect, and he set off for Holland and managed to gather facts and fictions on that country, its governors, people, and customs, material to be used in his provocative and much abused *Théorie des droits civils*. He returned to France, nearly choked with schemes, riddled with theories; and he pitched his perambulated tent for a while at Abbeville. Eventually, after further attempts at literature and poetry, his outburst against the philosophers in *Fanatisme des philosophes*, his Law diatribes, and his initiation among the advocates of the Parlement, since he had despaired of rising to eminence in Letters, he paid another momentous visit to Abbeville.

The town was in a fever of largely manufactured horror by reason of supposed atheism on the part of La Barre, a sprightly young chevalier, and three youthful friends; for they had not paid sufficient respect to ecclesiastical rites and authority, were accused of reading Voltaire, and, wrongfully, of sacrilege against a crucifix. The trial inflamed France, enraged Voltaire and his humane, bold fellows, and led to their fugitive reconciliation with Linguet; who, in view of his defending the Jesuits, might have been expected to abet the trumpeted charge against La Barre and his fellow-victims; whereas, actually, through Linguet's acquaintance Douville, leader of the liberal faction in the town and father of one of the juvenile culprits, to whom Linguet had served as a tutor, he took charge of the defence. Linguet, writing to Douville, said that before knowing his friend he had regarded solitude as the most gentle of aisles, hatred against men as the first of duties, and death as the most desirable of remedies for himself; and probably it was in gratitude to Douville that Linguet set his coruscating wits and his energies at work in support of the fancied atheists. He came too late to rescue La Barre, who was sentenced to the Question, to having his tongue plucked out and then his head struck off; but Linguet saved the rest of the accused; and, when public opinion inevitably reacted against the treacherous brutality of La Barre's death, Linguet sprang to fame as an advocate.

The tale of his complicated and interminable ragings

against his adversaries and for his numerous clients at the Bar, his association with the Duke d'Aiguillon and his exasperated quarrel with that august minister, his relation with the King and Madame du Barry, his unequalled popularity with the crowd and his embroilments with fellow-advocates, the Parlement, and many other persons and bodies; also his curious and comic, at first platonic, most learned love-affair with Madame Buttet, a client who became his sometimes tempestuous mistress and remained faithful to him until his death: all these facts, and a hundred others no less exciting or violent, must be sought in Cruppi's and other biographies of the indefatigable and perpetually querulous and always would-be sincere Linguet.

In 1775 he was entangled in a stiff network of vicious intrigues on the part of infuriated professional brethren, after his having become the editor of a journal of politics and literature, in which he scolded most things, and especially the Academy of Letters, expending and enjoying himself lustily in a kind of subsidiary line to his work as an advocate. He fought valorously, almost successfully, was defeated at last by cunning rather than by strength and integrity, and went into exile, struck off the rolls. Now began a new, more subtly belligerent, phase in the clamorous life of this unsubduable man.

At first he went to England, and his opponents hoped and assumed they had heard the last of him; and for a time little was in fact heard of him. He travelled here and there, storing his vexations, full-fraught with epithets, subsequently reached Brussels, and there founded his *Annales politiques civiles et littéraires*, something of a sequel to and an extension of his first journalistic work in Paris, from which he had been driven by police order. The *Annales* appeared at regular intervals, dribbled, then flowed in tide, over

Paris and elsewhere; and Linguet once more rose to a meridian of fame as he took rhetorical vengeance on his enemies, mingling himself, or rather his pen and corrosive ink, with all questions and events. The *Annales* were published abroad, and denounced in the Paris Parlement, the editor being accused of scandalizing Law, insulting the Tribunals, outraging the Bar, inciting Kings to despotism and the People to revolt. Linguet rejoiced exceedingly in his self-appointed, highly remunerative task of Job's Comforter and public censor. Meanwhile Authority could neither thwart nor gag him while he remained out of France; and Authority busied itself in sly effort to get him into France, having already—if he speaks truth—prepared the needful *lettre-de-cachet*.

The wiry little spitfire, naïvely confident in himself, swollen by success, anxious to parade himself and his success in Paris and inveigled thither by assurance of protection, fell plump into a trap. In September, 1780, when on his way, as he supposed, to dine with folk at Vincennes, he was startled, and soon disillusioned, to find his carriage surrounded by the Bastille-guard. He could not resist, and so spent his first night in prison, where he stayed for upwards of two years. His *Annales*, robbed temporarily of the Linguet-sting, continued to appear under the editorship of the proprietor's subordinates. Influences were launched in his favour at Court, he was released, and hurried to London, exacerbated, indignation glowing in him like the red heart of a fire; and promptly he poured out his woes, writing the Bastille *Mémoires*, soothed so far as he could be soothed in his moods by the loyal and devoted Madame Buttet, protected by her from interruption, worshipped by her—when they were not squabbling. The *Mémoires*, first printed in the *Annales*, then published separately, seem more or less true, though, written by a man nearly horn-made frequently they are emphatic to exaggeration; yet unquestionably Linguet sought to abide by the realities —and the success of the work rivalled the success of Latude's.

At length he returned to Paris, unmolested this time; for events were marching rapidly in France. He supported Camille Desmoulins and Danton, members of the revolutionary club of the Cordeliers; but his thought and his instincts and much of his life-work turned in the direction of a kindly despotism rather than toward a republic of any sort.   He continued to write against this and that, producing his journalistic squibs and rockets, pamphlets, and so on; until the excesses of the Revolution disheartened and nauseated him, and, with his always attendant Madame Buttet, he went into comparative retreat, having his small rural property not far from the village of Ville-d'Avray.   Here he commenced the last of his writings, a *Histoire de France*, maybe having wearied of his all but incessant struggles since youth, once again regarding solitude as the most gentle of aisles and hating men as a duty, while searching for peace and that philosophic calm ever more or less visualized, never realized. Then the capture of Louis XVI stirred him anew into movement, and, apparently, he wrote to the King, offering to plead for him as an advocate.

No doubt it was preordained that such a man as Linguet should be suspected when suspicion became the mode of the day; for, though doing much in his life-work to inflate the spirit of revolution, he had been a severely harsh critic of facts latterly embodied in the Revolution; and he too was haled before the Tribunals, accused of having encouraged tyranny and stock-jobbery, of flattering and offering to defend despots, and other items of the sort.   When he saw the act of arrest, he turned to his fellow-prisoners and smiled derisively, vowing he would make a fête of his trial and unmask the sottishness of his atrocious enemies: they should know what it meant to prosecute a Linguet. The Tribunal refused to hear him—he was condemned to death; and his fragmentary *Histoire de France* served the patriots for the manufacture of cartridges. "These men are not judges," he said as he returned to his cell; "they are tigers": which seems to have been the woefully ironical truth of it.

Linguet, for about thirty years of his nearly sixty years' life, had pranced and capered, and yelled with his piercing-shrill, menacing voice, using tricks without scruple to gain his ends against real and imaginary fools and knaves, caring not a rap for seemliness and deportment; but he died with courage and dignity, and in high Roman fashion. On his way to the scaffold he asked quietly for a priest, and, being refused, produced a copy of Seneca and solaced himself calmly to the end.

So perished Linguet as Revolution ravaged itself, fed on itself; so perished most of the heroes of that Revolution: Camille Desmoulins, Bailly the Mayor of Paris, Brissot, Fauchet, Manuel, and a host of others, went the way of the tumbrils; and many of those who sent them followed in turn. Thus until the young man Bonaparte, his grape-shot, unlike Broglie's, having got itself in and out of guns effectively, made end to horror for the moment; and he planted a new despotism on the smoking ruins of the old, spread slaughter, continuing until he too reached his appointed end; wherefore the Bourbons returned to rule France, or rather to attempt to rule France, this time without a Bastille.

J. M. W.

The Linguet *Mémoires*, like Latude's, are here translated from Barrière's edition of 1884. Monin, in his Linguet edition, followed the original text, as he says, more closely, restituting paragraphs

arbitrarily suppressed by Barrière. The latter, in his design to give
Memoirs of the Baſtille drawn from Latude and Linguet, excluded
what he considered irrelevant to the subjeᶜt, and, in the main, succeeded, producing a much more readable narrative. Linguet, in the
original, had added as mere Notes more than a third of his matter.
Barrière printed many of these Notes in their rightful place ; therefore
the work as it now ſtands makes a consecutive ſtory, and will doubtless
be preferred to Monin's edition by English readers intereſted primarily
in the Baſtille. Those, on the other hand, who are more direᶜtly
concerned with the man Linguet, muſt go to Monin—and to nearly
eighty volumes of Linguet's own works.—(*Tranſlator's Note.*)

MEMOIRS OF THE BASTILLE

AND OF THE AUTHOR'S DETENTION IN THIS ROYAL CHÂTEAU FROM SEPTEMBER 27, 1780, TO MAY 19, 1782

BY

SIMON NICOLAS HENRI LINGUET

" These unknown sufferings and obscure pains become useless to our justice the moment they no longer contribute through publicity and example to the maintenance of order."—*Declaration of Louis XVI, dated August 30th*, 1783.

London, December 5th, 1782.

ON September 27th, 1780, having been lured to Paris by a series of treacheries, some of which I shall disclose elsewhere, I was arrested in broad daylight, with deliberate, calculated infamy, and flung into dungeons apparently and solely reserved for enemies of the King, of religion, and the State. My person, my honour, and my fortune were delivered to every outrage within the range of infamous gaolers, unbridled slanderers, greedy fellows, and faithless agents.

My imprisonment seemingly came to an end on May 19th, 1782, and after a twenty months' lapse void of any sort of alleviation or explanation; whereas actually it only changed in form. The Paris lieutenant of police, who arrived in great state to tell me I was no longer a prisoner, added that I was exiled. He handed an order to me, banishing me to a small town forty leagues from Paris; and I was forbidden to leave this place *under penalty for disobedience*.

Although no explanation was offered concerning the motive either of my exile or of my imprisonment, and although I had the strongest reasons for supposing that this latest stroke came from the ministry and not from the King, yet I did not refuse to submit. I merely begged two quite simple favours: the one, permission to remain in Paris until I had at least recovered strength enough to betake myself thence, and had wrested the necessary means to live from the more than suspected hands which, by most curious means, had seized almost the whole of my property; the other, permission to spend several days at Brussels,

175

thus to terminate the confusion which, for two years, had been wasting the dregs of my fortune.

Furthermore, having returned to my existence, and with a new gift to bestow on my country, wishing practically to test a highly valuable invention, to realize for public benefit a fresh method of using light, one devised at a time when I saw no light,* assuredly I had the right to hope for, and to anticipate, a modification, even a revocation, of my exile.

Curiosity obtained a short delay for me on this count; nor was curiosity disappointed. I made the experiment, and with success! On that day they told me to *go to Rethel and to stay there* ; this despite the fact that, to obtain permission for the journey to Brussels, I had verbally and in writing given my word of honour to return immediately, and that for the past month I had continued to repeat my undertaking—one proffered already from the depth of my tomb, not, as some gazettes have stupidly or malignantly declared, *to write no more, save in accord with the views of the French ministry,* but never to write again, if that were demanded of me. I undertook to wrap myself in absolute silence, if in exchange for such a sacrifice at least the ordinary rights of a citizen should be restored to me; also that, if by necessity I resigned myself and ceased to serve society, I should not be treated more harshly than many other men who encumbered it. In addition, I made these requests and offers mildly and with a submission that seemed almost scandalous to impartial witnesses, and convinced several either that my spirit was subdued finally or that my mind had given way under excessive misfortune.

They deceived themselves; for my conduct at this time did not differ from the conduct maintained on

---

* The gift Linguet wished to bestow was a system of telegraphy, greatly improved on at a later date by the brothers Chappes, and more especially by the electric telegraph.—NOTE BY BARRIÈRE.

PLATE VI

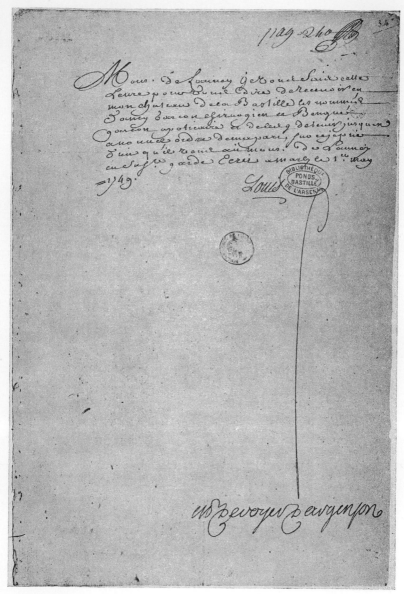

FACSIMILE OF A LETTRE DE CACHET

[face p. 176

all occasions throughout my life: never have I chosen noisy methods before exhausting all imaginable means to avoid them.

I thought of travelling for a few years: according to plan—and after doing homage at the feet of a prince,* who, by his example, gives such noble lessons to all princes and invests the throne of the Cæsars with a brilliance long unknown—I meant to visit Italy; where, studying the monuments of the past, I would strive to forget my sufferings in the present.

However, this indirect method of conforming to the views of the French ministry failed in effect. Faithful friends warned me that I was unpardoned because I had failed to impose a quite literal obedience on myself; and that, by means of ambushes strewing my way, the road to Italy would inevitably become a track to the Bastille for me.

Since this advice reached me by the same means as the warning of the *first lettre-de-cachet*—for I had been warned of this, though I had refused to believe—I realized the folly of risking a second. Consequently I put myself at an unbridgeable distance from the bounties of the French ministry. My true patrons, those who contributed to my safety, can certainly feel no displeasure at my having taken sure means of preserving the fruits of their friendship: if others show resentment, this resentment proves that such precautions were necessary.

To-day I ask all honest and impartial men if I could have done anything I did not do. Have I done anything I was not obliged to do?

At this point, and for the present, I shall not trench on a delicate subject, of which the discussion would be more laborious than the solution would be useful. I do not seek to know if State Prisons are a necessity of government; if all administration needs such deposi-

* Joseph II.

12

tories sheltered from legal inspection; if this violent and ever dangerous spring should be considered indispensable in machines which, to conserve themselves, must often suffer more than ordinary shocks; or finally if what is known in France by the fantastic name of *lettre-de-cachet* is a special malady peculiar to this kingdom—as plague to Egypt, small-pox to Arabia, or burning lava-floods to the neighbourhood of volcanoes; for this problem is in effect solved by the facts. If such a solution is inadmissible in humane philosophy, nevertheless it is adopted by *universal policy.*

No nation is discoverable where authority has not made use of this resource or of some equivalent. Rome, in the time of its most genuine liberty, had dictators. The orders of these supreme magistrates closely resembled *lettres-de-cachet*; for, without appeal or an account rendered, they controlled not only the freedom but the lives of citizens.

Reasons of State thrust despotism yet a step further in Sparta, so to speak. Even kings—that is to say, the heads of the nation—were thus subjected and could be sent to prison by the Ephors. This, in fact, was the contrary of a *lettre-de-cachet*; yet, actually, related to the species.

I see that in the quarter of the universe where administration is the most closely supervised and restricted, where they have succeeded notably in protecting persons without power from the arbitrary abuses of power—in London itself, a Tower exists for the incarceration of State criminals. Parliament, the guardian of private liberties, as of public privileges, not only shows no terror at the sight of a citadel apparently menacing one and the other, but sometimes makes use of it; nor does the Parliament, in acting thus, believe it violates or compromises the prerogatives of the people.

In mentioning the Tower of London and the Bastille

simultaneously, I should be unjustly, even criminally, reticent if I did not remark that the two abodes have more of a real difference between them than of a seeming resemblance. The officers of the Tower and the garrison at their command are submitted to parliamentary supervision, like all members of the State. A prisoner ill-treated has ample means of forwarding his complaints to superiors competent to redress them, and to friends and relations concerned to secure a hearing. The prisoner is certain that his case will be tried—and tried publicly. He has counsel and advocates; all points that must be cleared or deleted are communicated to him in the most abundant detail. The accusation of treason only determines the place where the prisoner shall be lodged and changes nothing whatsoever in the form of procedure that decides his fate; and finally, though this procedure may be severe and prolonged, there is never a shadow of doubt either as to the prisoner's existence—even in the matter of his health—or the place of his confinement. Is it thus in the Bastille?

Some punctilious censors, or members of the administration, will here perchance accuse me of extravagance; and possibly they will maintain that there are few countries where a fundamental equivalent to the Bastille cannot be found, where essentially yet more horrible measures and abuses do not take place: they will try by parallel to justify, at least indirectly, the abominable system I now denounce to all virtuous minds—a system which the most resolute partisan of tyranny would not dare to dream of excusing by such subterfuge.

Let us deprive them even of this resource. I agree that in almost every country the public good occasionally seems a sufficient excuse for legalizing extreme harshness; but it is untrue that the laws, or yet a continuous practice, have ever or elsewhere sanctioned

anything approaching the system of the Bastille. No
matter what the loathing this dire and shameful subject
inspires in me, no matter what disgust I feel at the
mere thought of protracting a necessary consideration
of it, let us rifle the annals of tyranny, survey the globe,
and discover if in the criminal history of arbitrary
power there are crimes that can be compared with the
institution of this fortress which dominates the Rue
Saint-Antoine at Paris.

This brief summary of bygone, unfamiliar woes will
perhaps make a deeper impression than the most vivid
description of our own miseries. When a modern
Titus considers the effect of *lettres-de-cachet* in all ages,
comparing them with the results yet produced in our
time, he will more easily decide whether it be expedient
for him to continue the use of such things, or to spur
himself in rivalry with such men as Phalaris and Nero.

Therefore I repeat—and I will prove this by facts—
that in the entire universe there has never been anything
resembling the system of the Bastille. We can find
no nation blighted by the shame and inhumanity of a
permanent Bastille; of a pit always gaping to receive
men, not for *punishment*—let this be fully borne in
mind—but for *torture* : a political purgatory, where the
most trivial faults, and often innocence itself, may be
subjected arbitrarily to the torments of hell.

Throughout antiquity we find State Prisons alone
at the command of the most abominable of tyrants,
and only during their reigns. These prisons were
temporary scourges, like sword or poison, used by
execrable oppressors while usurpation lasted, disappearing with them; they formed no part of the
country's constitution, nor were they among the
favourite weapons of a government, nor used habitually
as a resource of authority. From what we know of
their organization, they cannot be compared in any
sense with the Bastille.

For example, we read that the first Dionysius had a similar prison in his palace at Syracuse, and that there, says history, a refinement was practised which, it is perhaps astonishing to discover, remained unadopted by any of the lesser Dionysiuses who followed in his footsteps so successfully, perfecting the Bastille system. The vaulted dungeon-roofs were curved so artfully that every spoken word re-echoed and could be heard distinctly in a chamber devised as a receptacle for these collected sounds. This was the observatory, or, more accurately, the confessional where the tyrant established himself, so to intercept the secrets and conversations of the prisoners: an ingenious chamber named *The Ear*

Nevertheless, *The Ear* was not all-hearing; for it is related that a philosopher, having been imprisoned on a *lettre-de-cachet* and subsequently released, roused the curiosity of the tyrant, who wanted to learn from him how captives passed their time. " By wishing for your death," said the candid prisoner. Hence *The Ear* had not revealed this secret; one resulting—if the story is to be credited—in another *lettre-de-cachet* containing an order to slice the throats of all the prisoners. Whatever may or may not be the truth of this last stroke, the fact remains that, since *The Ear* was constructed to catch the talk of prisoners, they could talk together and see one another, and were not abandoned to an absolute solitude; therefore it was not the Bastille.

Among the Romans we find neither *Ear* nor Bastille. During the time of the Republic, even guilty citizens usually forestalled arrest—since it was not permitted until after condemnation—by a voluntary exile; and innocence had yet greater assurance against despotic imprisonment.

Under the Emperors, however, innocence was not beyond the reach of assassination by royal command;

but, at that time, the sacrifice took place actually in the homes of the victims. The *lettre-de-cachet*, countersigned Sejanus, Narcissus, Tigellinus, and so on, and embodying the death-warrant, was notified by a tribune and a centurion in charge of a squad of soldiers.

At sight of the ministerial order, a number of men took poison, some stabbed themselves with daggers, and others opened their veins; and the troops, having surrounded the house until the completion of the business, returned casually to their barracks, as if they were merely coming off guard.

The cry will certainly be raised that this was considerably more harsh than a Bastille system. I cannot say. This strange problem can be solved alone by captives in that prison. Judging for myself, and from my own experience, the prompt method of a Roman despot seems infinitely preferable. A thousand times I begged by word of mouth and in writing for prosecution or death; and in those days the bath of Seneca or the dagger of Thraseas would have seemed a favour to me.

However, without pronouncing on this question, it is yet and at least clear to me that these Narcissus-folk did not begrudge the comfort of making a will ere death to men of whom they wished to rid themselves. Such tolerance, in fact, was the reward of a prompt obedience: the power to draw up final depositions and the certainty that they would be fulfilled were, according to Tacitus, *pretium festinandi*. Unquestionably, in the Bastille, a like resignation and the proximity of a death hastened by my vows did not bring to me any indemnity of the sort. Therefore the balance is unequal. At Rome, in similar instances, death was more certain; whereas, in France, approach to death was made more dolorous.

Furthermore, this murderous Roman haste was to be dreaded solely by the nobles; and, as a rule, the monsters who exacted it did not escape from public vengeance. Sejanus was torn to shreds by the people; Nero, proscribed by decrees, would have perished in ignominious torture had he not taken his own life. In addition, Trajans and Antonines came periodically to deliver Rome from opprobrium and to check the practices which, otherwise and in time, might have become the prerogatives of the crown.

One sees that under the worst of sovereigns, State criminals, or rather, ordinary State prisoners, were only subjected to an uncomfortable restraint, and not to hideous captivity. They were attached by one hand to the hand of a soldier, who, in consequence, could not leave them. Doubtless this was an unpleasant partnership; but it did not prevent Agrippa from sleeping peacefully at home in the time of Tiberius, nor St Paul from public preaching in the time of Nero. Was this like the Bastille ?

The single example we find of a rigorous State Prison maintained continuously in ancient Rome was what they called Transportation. Persons who had become suspicious to the Court were removed to small uninhabited islands; and here they were abandoned, under a strict death-penalty if they left the place. I admit that one does not see how ordinary procedure could justify such *lettres-de-cachet*; but, anyhow, the unfortunate creatures thus degraded enjoyed the light of day and the possibility of breathing fresh air; they retained part of their incomes, they might have some of their servants with them; they wrote and received letters; finally, if tedium grew unbearable and they preferred expatriation to shameful resignation, they could escape; and they did escape. Thus once more, and clearly, this was not yet the Bastille.

The history of the Lower Empire being far from exact, it is impossible to follow specifically and in detail the jurisprudence of *lettres-de-cachet*. Would-be Emperors were often made and unmade with as little ceremony as the Deys of Algeria, hence their ministers could barely have found time to make State Prisons subserve vengeance; and instead of cooping their victims, they cut their throats forthwith—a procedure often adopted even by those who enjoyed a prosperous and brilliant reign.

Constantine had his own system whereby persons of whom he wished to rid himself without noise or scandal were suffocated in hot baths: thus his wife, his son, and others. In addition, he had his father-in-law strangled, his brother beheaded, and he behaved gently with none save the bishops, content to exile them: apparently he did not imprison anyone.

It is possible to conjecture that, under the reign of his son Constantius, the foundations of a Bastille were laid; for, since there was a certain disturbance in a council held by his order, when the Fathers differed to a pitch of violence, provincial commandants holding *lettres-de-cachet* imprisoned a few members; one of whom, Lucifer, wrote directly to the Emperor, saying: " . . . . Because we withdrew from your council of iniquity, we languish in prison, deprived of the sun's light, kept closely in darkness; nor is anyone allowed to come to us. . . ." Here, indeed, is the likeness of a Bastille.

Nevertheless, on the one hand, we see that the prelate had permission to address himself straightway to the sovereign, complaining to him of the harshness of his detention; whereas this is precisely one of the things explicitly forbidden in Bastille codes. On the other hand, no doubt, if such an admirable contrivance had been once admitted to the Empire, it must have remained in perpetuity—wherefore no need to wait until the age of Louis XI for its revival; but there are no further traces of such a thing discoverable in Constantinople. When they wanted to get rid of

Saint John Chrysostom, he was sent to Cucuse, and instead of being killed by immobility in a dungeon, he perished through excessive journeying; nor, seemingly, did the thought occur to them of burying him in a citadel, where he would have been regarded as dead while yet alive.

The secretaries of State and their clerks under the Grecian Empire realized at an early date the importance to them of destroying the sight of men whom they judged worthy such resentful attention, but never did they contrive vaults built in walls twenty or thirty feet thick. Instead of obscuring sight, they attacked the eyes directly by plucking them out, roasting them with red-hot copper or silver wires, or by drenching them with boiling vinegar; and all in virtue of a *lettre-de-cachet*.

I admit that these State criminals were blinded, yet the tyranny thus martyrizing them was no law of the State; there was no minister at Court with a special department for the blinding of prisoners. In Constantinople the lieutenant of police was not deputed by precise warrant to be the imperial commissioner for the application of fiery vinegar or red-hot instruments.

In modern Constantinople—this blot on our so-called philosophy, this scandal of the human race—there is a fortress which seems to have some affinity with the Bastille; the fortress of the Seven Towers. Travellers call it a State Prison; but, by reason of their own accounts, one recognizes that it is a *dépôt* rather than a prison. Scarcely anyone except Christian ambassadors of Powers who break with the Porte are consigned to it; and they continue not only to see whom they please, but to be attended by their own servants.

Slaves whose ransom is agreed on though not yet paid are sometimes obliged to go thither to await the completion of the bargain; and therefore it is at once a refuge for them and a guarantee for their masters. These slaves, idle, well-fed, and visited frequently, wear no fetters, and already anticipate the flavour of liberty.

Authority, however, would not dare to confine in the Seven Towers men against whom no crime had been imputed, and who must merely languish there, more rigorously sequestered than the most infamous of villains. Neither Sultan, Vizier, Cadi, nor Janissary has ever thought of giving, soliciting or executing a *lettre-de-cachet* against a bourgeois of Constantinople, Erzerum, or Salonica, because he found the Grand Vizier's diamond cluster less brilliant than usual or the slipper of the *Séliâar* ill-embroidered.

If a blasphemer insults the Prophet, he is impaled or circumcized: the law is clear, and at least he can make a choice. When a Vizier has abused his power he is exiled or despoiled, sometimes strangled: why did he show himself so grasping? for what purpose was he made Vizier? If a baker sells short weight and so robs the public, he is punished as a thief, and such punishment is swift, often terrible; but the offence and the conviction must be established beforehand. All the inhabitants of this vast Empire—Greeks, Armenians, Franks, Asiatics, Europeans, Tartars, Catholics, Schismatics, Copts, Jews, Mussulmans—pass their days in the most peaceful and the most happy security, if they observe the laws; specifically if they are fortunate enough to be unknown to the seraglio. They have no conception whatsoever of a Bastille or of a *lettre-de-cachet*.

In Persia, throughout the period of its splendour and tranquillity—that is, before the civil wars which devastated it for half a century—not only were these resources of ministerial vengeance equally unknown, but even ordinary justice found means to spare persons rightly suspected from the humiliation and horror of dungeons. The prisons there were mobile. When public order demanded that a man should be arrested, he was deprived solely of that degree of freedom which would enable him to evade punishment or to extend his crime. The *cangue* had been invented, and by an ingenuity more compassionate than severe: a kind of portable, wooden triangle which, fitted around the neck and securing one of the accused man's hands, prevented him from hiding or disengaging himself, though he was not deprived of any other faculty. Accordingly, as he carried his own inexpensive guard, he could enjoy daylight, lead his own life, administer his affairs, and, without ceasing to be submissive to the civil power, had every needful facility for demonstrating his innocence, which this power must verify.

We hear of bloody executions ordered by drunken monarchs, but these horrors took place in the harems; and the institution of the *cangue* proves in itself that the general spirit of the nation, not excepting the government, was characterized alike by mildness and equity.

So it is in Mongolia, in all the Indies, and in China and Japan. Accounts reaching us from the latter country —whence our restlessness has justly caused our banishment—assert that the customs are cruel, the punishments as prompt as they are terrible. This may be true: anyhow, swiftness in some respects counterbalances barbarity, and there are no long confinements perpetuating that most dreadful of tortures—despair evoked by doubt concerning the end of torment.

The man who is disembowelled, flung on to spikes, minced into ten thousand pieces, brayed alive in a mortar—if it be true that such subtleties of torture are common—has had a trial, able to defend and to justify himself: he is condemned by law and a magistrate, not by caprice.

Occasionally our missionaries have been lodged in

the prisons of India. Unknown strangers preaching novelties which certainly appeared curious even to the most indifferent of appraisers and criminally dangerous to the magistrates, and especially so to the priests, whose declared enemies our missionaries were—these men would seem with a more genuine and lawful excuse to merit harsh treatment and *lettres-de-cachet* ; yet they have been impelled to do justice to the humanity of the judges who imprisoned them, to the gaolers who guarded them, to the natives of the country who visited, consoled, and nourished them.

We can find no example analogous to our royal châteaux or to the orders populating them, except in the adventure of blood-princes baptized by Jesuits, first exiled, then imprisoned under the Emperor Iontching. The missionaries who tell us of this catastrophe have not revealed the cause; but, whatever it may have been, their story establishes clearly the fact that there were no Bastilles in China, since a Bastille had to be constructed expressly for each of the princes destined to submission therein.

Even then there were no clandestine abductions effected secretly by officers of the police, provoking similar doubts as to the lives, the guilt, or innocence of the prisoners. These temporary prisons were erected with great pomp and carefully placed in full sight as an example of high punishment, the object of which was doubtless known throughout the countryside.

Yet nevertheless, in the midst of this frightful harshness, the criminals enjoyed some relief: they saw their servants on occasion; they could demand spiritual assistance from their guides, the authors of their misfortune; food, clothing, also news, was carried to them from their homes—in short, all things scrupulously excluded from the Bastille.

In the whole of Asia it is impossible to discover a definite State Prison forming a constituent part of government—except in Ceylon. "There," says a traveller, "the King has numerous prisoners confined, some in ordinary prisons, others in charge of his lords. No one would dare to inquire why they are there, or when they were sent thither; and they are kept thus for five or six years. All imprisonment is by order of the King. . . ."

Here in effect are traces of the Bastille; and the mysteries of State in Ceylon approximate slightly to those of the Rue Saint-Antoine. Observe, however, that there is no question of dungeons contrived especially to entomb miserable men about whose crime or calamity silence is so urgently prescribed. They are assigned to the ordinary prisons or confided to the care of noblemen.

Consequently, in the first instance, they suffer a misfortune common to all accused persons; in the second, probably they find mitigations of all sorts in their private yet royal prison-houses. One cannot suppose that the entire nobility of Colombo or Kandy develop the characteristics of a Bastille governor, thus because a despot demands a temporary assumption of such duties. And it is obvious that none of these swarthy gentlemen have either iron-laced windows and chimneys in their houses, or walls thirty feet thick, or chambers which are prisons within prisons and cause an incessant alternation between misery and shame.

Evidently, therefore, the whole of Asia is exempt from this pestilence which consumes so many citizens in France.

In America there are many other kinds of oppression, likewise in Africa; but this particular species is un- known. The Indians of the New World are crushed by pitiless masters, themselves debased by superstition. A section of the African coast is submissive to despotic government, one displaying only the dangers and abuses of the government that controls Asia. The rest, apparently, is devastated solely by our commerce; for it is not the African princes, but rather the merchants of Europe, who impose chains on the inhabitants of Congo and Juida. These creatures are sold, doomed to a life of active labour; but no minister has the right to condemn them at his good pleasure to a deathly inertia. Unquestionably they are miserable in their Antillean huts, but with a different misery, one admitting comforts and alleviations, since they have their wives and children. Exactitude in a fulfilment of their tasks may save them from the overseer's lash; but no one has ever been saved by this means from a *lettre-de-cachet* and its consequences.

Hence these terrible flails are formidable only in Europe; and yet, where in Europe are they to be feared? Not in Great Britain, as one knows. Arbitrary inprisonment in that country would be high-treason against the people, punishable almost as severely as high-treason against the King; and I have already paid homage to the not less well-known truth that, in examples of imprisonment which superior interests and conditions affecting the public service authorize, the accused man, even the guilty prisoner, loses none of the rights or resources of innocence.

In Germany princes are generally despotic enough, in the usual sense of that word—namely, no actual barrier constrains either the use or the abuse of their power. Notwithstanding, they have no Bastille, nor an equivalent. There is nothing to prevent them from indulging in this amusement; but whether the notion occurs only to ministers of large States, or whether recourse to the Emperor and the existing tribunals and the fear of granting too great an influence to these bugbears—who, indubitably, would lose no possible opportunity of signalizing themselves—restrains the owners of these great fiefs; or whether the people, ever patient, docile, and usually as uneducated as they are unimpassioned, obey readily enough without subjection to such yoke, it seems to me that no Bastille exists from the Rhine to the Oder, except at Spandau. However, and primarily, Spandau has its existence in a monarchy which is entirely military; for this Colossus, arisen in our time and having reached a forced development as astonishing as it was swift, must preserve something of its origin in its constitution. On the other hand, this Brandenburgian Bastille is especially and specifically devoted to the soldiery. Citizens very rarely share such a baleful honour; and can soldiers, who recognize no spokesman except cannon or bayonet, complain if sometimes they are answered by *lettres-de-cachet* ?

In Denmark, since the time of the abominable Christiern, I find no trace of Kings or ministers who were tempted to start these *lettres-de-cachet* ; nor do Jutland and Fionia groan under such a deadly, useless mass as a Bastille. In Sweden no King has defiled his reign with the order to construct or to use a like place.

Finally, in Russia, the country among all others in the world where ancient customs would have been most compatible with Bastillery and its attributes, precisely the contrary practices are established. *Lettres-de-cachet* flourish in full vigour, but the consequences are utterly different; for there an entire province has become a State Prison. In France part of a prisoner's torment is the smallness of the prison; in Siberia they bewail only its immensity. The French are entombed in veritable graves; the Russians are lost in a great desert. However miserable the latter may be, yet undoubtedly they are less to be pitied, having compensations and distractions: they are followed or accompanied by their families; and though their hearts may be often sore when they recall their losses one to another, yet they can comfort themselves with and exercise themselves in what remains. At least they can weep together; whereas the only real, bitter tears are those shed in solitude. Moreover, the active life they are forced to lead preserves them from the weariness and from the torment of turning incessantly to the past, or of trembling in apprehension of what the future may hold for them. Doubtless they are indeed miserable; but they would not think so if they knew the Siberia of France.

In Spain, I believe, there are two or three towers created by the ministry among a number of governmental devices and State necessities; but these towers are almost empty, for, until a recent date, they have been rivalled by the prisons of the Inquisition. A people who will bear this latter yoke, and bear it placidly, cannot serve as a term of comparison in any consideration of policy relative to the former governmental yoke.

In Italy, as in Germany, Inquisition prisons are nearly unknown. In Rome and Venice, however, indications exist of a formidable government and a clearly defined Bastillage. There is a castle in the one, a tribunal in the other; alike ever-ready weapons for despotism, and equally outrageous to justice. Nevertheless, the host of foreigners constantly traversing these famous countries proves that the use of such things is less frequent than the alarming apparatus would suggest. When Englishmen or Hamburgers set out for Rome to hear oratorios, to admire St Peter's, or to dance at a masked ball in Venice, their families never tremulously implore them to beware of the ancient castle of Hadrian, or of the State Inquisition; whereas every foreigner who declares that he means to go to France is warned to be on his guard against the Bastille.

Suppose we were to read in the accounts of travels— which in these latter years have increased so plenteously by reason of a transitory restlessness—that in austral regions, in some of those islands seemingly hidden by nature from the rest of the world, there exists a nation gay, mild, and quite frivolous, whose government is not eager to shed blood, where the most serious business always takes a sportive turn; where a bottomless pit, however, is carefully preserved in the chief city into which all citizens without exception may be hurled at any moment: some, in fact, are thus hurled daily, by orders impossible to avoid, of which there is no hope of investigating, nor, often, of guessing either the pretext or the motive.

Suppose that the wretched man who vanishes in this way finds himself separated from the entire world, more distant from his relatives, friends, and especially from justice, than if he had been transferred to a distant planet; also that his complaints are stifled without redress, or, rather, have one solitary channel for issue; a channel solely concerned to suppress complaints in proportion as their cause—the oppression inciting them—is more palpable, more grave.

Suppose this man to be abandoned, at least for a long period, without books, without papers, and unable to communicate with anyone, meanwhile tortured by his ignorance of all outside events, of what happens to his family, *his fortune or his honour*, of the matter of his accusation or the fate reserved for him— a torture more acutely stimulated, more deeply felt, by reason of a solitude unrelieved by any sort of distraction.

Suppose he has no other pledge for the surety of his life than the susceptibility of his keepers who, in spite of the *honourable order* attached to their apparel,* are capable of degrading themselves for cash, becoming vile satellites at the beck of an arbitrary command; who would certainly be unreluctant to assume yet more dastardly and barbarous functions at a like price, if

* Cross of the Order of Saint-Louis.

13

such things were required of them. Under these
conditions the prisoner may not unreasonably spy
death in all the food served to him; and the dismal
creak of heavy bolts whenever his door opens may seem
a presage of his death-sentence, a signal for the appearance of mutes destined to accomplish it. In addition,
knowledge of his own innocence, or of the natural
justice of his sovereign, cannot induce tranquillity, since
the first abuse of justice may be followed by a second,
since the rights over his liberty extend also to his life,
since the hands lending themselves a thousand times a
day to his moral assassination by virtue of a *lettre-de-
cachet* would doubtless at any time agree to kill him
physically, acting on authorization; for every assault
can be committed and hidden with a like facility in a
place where all is pain and mystery.

If the prisoner keeps his health, this is merely an
added torture; for his sensibilities are more keen, his
privations more grievous. If his health gives way, as
almost always happens, the immutable system of the
place delivers him helpless and comfortless to the
thought—dreadful, unshunnable—that his ashes will
be robbed of the last tribute paid by affection to a
beloved one lost, and that in all likelihood his death will
remain unknown; that his wife and his deluded children
will yet make vows and strive to deliver him, long
after the tomb in which he was buried alive contains
nothing but his *fleshless bones*.

If any such descriptions were discovered in the
Voyages of Cook or of the Admiral Anson, what would
our impression be? Should we not read them as the
tales of an impostor, flattering ourselves because we
lived in a country exempt from such bondage? Should
we not conceive a mistrust mingled with horror for a
government so barbarous, a nation so dishonoured?

Alas! this is a description of the Bastille; and it is
yet short of the truth! How faintly it suggests the

soul-tortures, the prolonged frenzies, the ever-recurrent anguish eternalizing the pains of death without ever attaining its repose—all, indeed, that the gaolers of the Bastille could impose in the way of indescribable suffering!

The first article of their code is the impenetrable mystery that enshrouds all their operations, a mystery reaching so far as to obscure not only the *residence*, but the *existence* of the man who has disappeared into their hands; a mystery not restricted to the forbidding of all and every access to him, of news likely to comfort or to divert him, but which likewise prevents anyone from verifying his whereabouts, or even whether *he is alive*.

A Bastille officer, when questioned in the world outside about a man he meets and ill-treats day by day, will shamelessly maintain that he has neither seen nor known him. When my true friends besought permission to see me from the minister in charge of these *oubliettes*, he answered with the air of one astonished because anybody could possibly believe that I might be in the Bastille. The governor often vowed to several of my friends, and on his *honour*, his *faith as a gentleman*, that I was no longer in the Bastille, having remained there less than a week; for the scandal of my arrest, the care taken to effect this in full daylight and on the open road, did not allow him to insist, as otherwise he would have done, that I had never been there at any time.

A lackey fables thus at his master's door and at his master's bidding, though only in order to avoid unseasonable visits: his lies serve a useful end or an agreeable purpose; he neither overlays them with affectation nor with oaths; yet he is degraded by this service. And now reflect on the conduct of a minister, or of a governor of the Bastille, who deceives merely to torment and whose lies result in nothing but misery!

What, I ask boldly, is the object of this feigned uncertainty, this deceiving an entire public, friends and family, as to the physical existence of a man who has been ravished from them ? This can in no way tend to enforce his conviction or to assure his chastisement; because, firstly, such mystery adds nothing to other accredited means either for investigating the charges against the prisoner, or for carrying out his punishment —if this has ever been pronounced; secondly, my example proves that the Bastille often harbours men against whom not only is there no desire to bring an action, but against whom no action could be brought; and, in particular, it is about the fate of such men that the deepest mystery is assumed. I repeat: to what end ?

Since the system of this prison is designed expressly to harrow the soul, to *make life bitter*—as one of those cross of Saint-Louis torturers, unabashed by these duties, once said to me naïvely—I can understand that complete isolation, and the invariable ignorance in which the prisoner is kept about what has been done, is being done, or will be done against him, is a means exactly in line with the end proposed: nothing could be better imagined to make a man endure all grades of despair, especially if he has the misfortune to possess the active, proud mind of those who are revolted by any hint of injustice, and for whom occupation is essential and the act of waiting a torment. But why should his kinsmen and his friends share this torment, when a pretence is made of not wishing to involve them in his misfortunes ?

When an action is brought, one knows at least the nature of the accusation and the limits to which it may be carried; the course of the prosecution may be followed; the victim is in view until the moment of sacrifice or of triumph; anxiety has limits and grief its consolations.

Here, however, while the unhappy, hidden wretch accuses his friends and family of forgetfulness, they tremble lest their regard for him should be criminal. Since his captivity depends on caprice, his chains may be removed at any hour, or perpetuated without end; therefore, to him and to those who hope for his return, each day is an entire cycle embodying all the anguish of expectation and all the horror of privation. At dawn they bemoan the thought of all that has been endured, and at night the certainty of renewed suffering; they cannot glimpse a likely end to the wretchedness, and new heartbreak is the solitary result if the imagination seeks to envisage such an end.

In the design of the original founder of the Bastille, this dreadful policy had reason: he wished to rid himself without noise or scandal of men for whose murder the executioner would have refused to act. When this founder proscribed an innocent man—for only the innocent were thus condemned, the guilty being tried—when he proscribed an innocent man, he determined that the time appointed for execution should remain unknown so that he might arrange it at a precise moment agreeable to his interests or to *his vengeance.*

But Louis XVI is not Louis XI, the first being as compassionate as the other was inhuman, the one alike respecting justice and law, enjoining their observance with as much care as the other took to gratify himself by violating them and by setting the example of infraction. How, then, does it come to pass that under the benevolence of Louis XVI the system invented by the tyranny of Louis XI is yet preserved? Why, under a sovereign to whom justice is dear and the blood of men is precious, are his subjects exposed to disasters similar to those under a sovereign for whom an execution was a charming spectacle, one who called his executioner his *crony*, and who never went abroad save under the escort of a satellite, likewise his crony, but more fierce and cruel than all executioners in a bunch ?

Furthermore, if it were the gravity of the crime or the character of the person that determined this strange and perilous incognito—if only men condemned to an approaching punishment because of the enormity of their crimes, or intriguers made formidable by birth, riches, or connections, had been shrouded in this sepulchral veil—then at least there would have been a pretext or an excuse.

The Bastille, however, like death, levels all it swallows: the sacrilegist contemplating the ruin of his country; the man of courage, guilty alone of defending his country with too much ardour; the coward who traffics with State secrets, also he who utters truths wholesome though contrary to the interests of ministers; the man confined because his crimes might compromise his family and the man feared merely for his talent—all are engulfed in the same darkness.*

Think well on this! the darkness is twofold and hinders sight and the being seen. It not only deprives the captive of all knowledge that might interest him personally and of the power of regulating his affairs, thus by provisional or definite arrangement preventing his own ruin and sometimes the ruin of his correspondents; above all, of the power to instruct his patrons and to disarm his enemies—in short, of everything that might occupy him usefully—but it even hides from him the review of public affairs that might distract

* This is not quite accurate. . . . I do not pretend that there were no exceptions : I speak of the *general system*, of my personal experience and of what I heard unceasingly about the usual custom and everyday life of the place, above all, one feels, fatal to the innocent. When harshness is dictated by caprice, only *patronage can secure dispensation ;* but immediately an innocent man is shut in the Bastille, it becomes clear either that he has no patron, or that his patrons are less powerful than his enemies. Therefore the abominable system in question is prepared expressly for him.

him. He is a stranger to the whole universe, nor may he so much as inquire about what is happening in the outside world. Perchance there may be a man in the dungeons who day by day importunes Louis XV and the Duke de la Vrillière with his supplications, mean-while believing he is imprisoned by them; he kneels continuously before two phantoms, creatures who, except in memory, have long ago ceased to exist; and the prison officials, witnesses of his mistake, do not enlighten him, because of their stupid squeamishness or base scruples.

From this active and passive ignorance the most disastrous effects result for the wretched man so de-ceived. If, for example, he has only been sacrificed to the personal vengenace of some fellow in office, he is not relieved even by the fall of the colossus whose prosperity has crushed him. He can gain no advan-tage for himself, since he is not informed of the event. If he has no zealous friends, if his family is timid or obscure, indifferent or far away, the oppression does not cease, though the oppressor may have disappeared. The successor thinks of employing like expedients rather than of redressing wrongs already provoked by them. The prisoner remains in the Bastille, not because anyone desires that he should be there, but because he is there—and, since the authorities are unsolicited, he is forgotten: hence nothing equals the difficulty of issuing from this deadly gulf, except the facility of falling into it.

The prelude, when fresh prey is brought forward, is the *search*. This taking possession of a prisoner's person, the method of establishing an infernal pro-prietorship in which he is about to be included, consists in despoiling him of all that may belong to him. He is equally afraid and astonished when he finds himself handed over to an examination by, and the fumblings of, four men whose appearance seems to belie their duties and makes them seem only the more shameful; four men dressed in a uniform—one inspiring a hope of respect—and wearing an honourable order which, I must repeat, presupposes an unblemished service.

They take away the prisoner's money, fearing otherwise he may use it to corrupt someone among themselves; his jewels follow, for a similar reason; his papers, lest he may find a resource against the tedium they wish to impose on him; his scissors, knife, and so on, because they declare they are afraid he might cut his own throat or murder his gaolers—for they calmly explain the motive of all their depredations. After this ceremony—lengthy and often interrupted by pleasantries and comments on every object entered in the inventory—they lead the prisoner to the den allotted to him in this menagerie.

These dens are all fashioned in the tower walls, which, as I have said, are at least twelve feet thick, and have thirty or forty solid feet at the base. Each one has a solitary loophole pierced in the masonry and obstructed by three iron gratings, one inside, the second midway, the third at the outer edge of the wall. The bars are crossed, being a square inch thick; and, by a subtlety that proves the superiority of the inventor's genius, the solid part of each of these queer gratings corresponds exactly with the opening in its neighbour, thus barely leaving a two-inch passage for the sight, though the lozenges measure almost four inches across.

Formerly, each of these vaults had two or three openings, certainly quite small, and decorated with the same network; but, finally, so many windows let too much fresh air into the place. A most humane governor had them blocked, leaving one only; in consequence, on the finest day, the fraction of light filtering in merely serves the better to enforce gloom.

Thus in winter these fatal vaults are ice-houses, being sufficiently raised to allow a penetration of cold;

PLATE VII

Vue De la Bastille de Paris De la porte St Antoine et D'une partie Du fauxbourg St Antoine

VIEW OF THE BASTILLE AND THE ST. ANTOINE GATE

[face p. 200

and in summer they are humid stoves where one is suffocated because the walls are too thick ever to be dried by heat.

Several of them, including mine, open directly on to the moat where the great drain from the Rue Saint-Antoine discharges itself; accordingly, when the drain is cleared out, or in summer after a sequence of hot days, or after the floods—an occurrence frequent enough during spring and autumn, and with moats sunk below the level of the river—a putrid stench arises; which, once drawn into these pigeonholes called rooms, dissipates itself very slowly.

Such is the atmosphere breathed by a prisoner; and here, in order to avoid being thoroughly suffocated, he is obliged to pass days, and often nights, glued against the inner grating that separates him, as I have said above, from the hole cut in the shape of a window and through which air and a shadow of daylight filters to him. His efforts to suck a little fresh air through this narrow pea-shooter often serve only to thicken the suffocating fetidness about him.

Woe betide the unhappy man who, in winter, cannot raise sufficient money to supplement the wood distributed in the King's name. At one time this was given without stint or reckoning, and in proportion to the consumption of each prisoner. They did not haggle with men—men otherwise deprived of all things and reduced to such a cruel immobility—over the amount of fire needful to uncurdle blood torpid through inaction, or to disperse the vapours condensed on the walls. The King ordained that they should enjoy this mitigation or distraction, and without restricting the expense.

Doubtless the intention is yet the same, but the methods have changed. The present governor has fixed the wood-consumption of each recluse to six logs, large or small. Everybody knows that, in Paris, logs for the house are half the size of logs for commercial purposes, since they are sawn through the middle, being only eighteen inches long. The economical distributor takes care that choice shall be made from the thinnest pieces found in the wood-yard, and—a fact as incredible as it is true—the worst pieces. By preference he has the base of piles and waste wood from shops selected, stuff despoiled of all salts by damp or age, and, for this reason, offered at a low price to workfolk such as brewers or bakers, who need a clear rather than a substantial fire. Six of these match-sticks make up the twenty-four hours' provision for inmates of the Bastille.

It may be asked what happens when this provision is exhausted. Prisoners do as they are told in abrupt terms to do by the honest governor: they suffer.

The furniture is in harmony with the light falling on it, and with the lair it is intended to adorn. Note, in the first place, that the governor, according to his contract with the ministry, must provide and keep the furniture in order, and at his own expense: this is one of the very small charges imposed on his immense income, of which I shall speak presently. He can excuse the inconveniences of the abode, since he cannot change the position of the premises; he can palliate the odious stinginess, mentioned above, exercised by him over the supply of wood, using the pretext that this tends to reduce the King's expenses; but in the matter of furniture, concerning himself alone, and for which he is paid, there is neither excuse nor palliation. His economies of the sort are necessarily and alike a cruelty and a theft.

Thus the inventory, certainly of my supply, comprised two moth-eaten mattresses, a cane chair with a seat only held together by string, a folding table, a water-crock, two earthenware pots—one being for

drink—and two stone slabs to support the fire. After
several months I obtained tongs and a fire-shovel, by
means of a compassionate turnkey. Fire-dogs I could
not get; and—either by policy, or inhumanity—if the
governor did not himself choose to supply a thing, he
determined that the prisoner should not have it at his
own expense. I could not achieve the purchase of a
teapot until eight months had passed: it took me twelve
months to procure with my own money an ordinary,
solid arm-chair, and fifteen months elapsed before I
could replace with common crockery the dirty and
disgusting pewter plates alone circulating in the
establishment.

In the early days, the solitary article I bought by
permission was a woollen blanket. The occasion arose
as follows.

The month of September, as everyone knows, is
the season when eggs of the maggots that fret woollen
stuffs are transformed into moths. Immediately the
den assigned to me had been opened, there arose from
the bed not a swarm, not a cloud, but a wide, thick
column of these insects: it expanded, quickly inundated
the place. I drew back, horrified.

"All right, all right!" said one of the men who
accompanied me, smiling. "There won't be one
left when you've slept here two nights."

In the evening the lieutenant of police came to
welcome me, according to custom. I showed such
extreme repugnance at the squalid, swarming bed that,
actually, I was allowed to get a new blanket and to
have the mattresses beaten, all at my own expense.
I wished to have these wretched mattresses renovated
in such fashion every three months, since feather-beds
are forbidden in the Bastille, no doubt because luxuries
of the sort are not suitable for men to whom the ministry
particularly wishes to give lessons in abstinence. The
governor-proprietor opposed me strenuously, although

it would have cost him nothing; he declared that the like treatment wore out mattresses.

Madame de Staal narrates that she had some tapestry hung in her room. Whether she owed this condescension to her position as the favourite of a great princess, or whether the customs of the Bastille at that time yet retained something of humanity—as other details of her captivity suggest—I do not know. Anyhow, and unquestionably, indulgences of this kind are one of the irregularities suppressed by a modern observance of rules. My requests to be permitted at my own expense to have either canvas, which would have helped to absorb the moisture from the walls, while hiding their lugubrious colour, or paper to produce the same effect—with the additional advantageous diversion of hanging it myself—were all futile.

There was something frightful about the appearance of the walls in my chamber. One of my predecessors, apparently an artist or an amateur, and less strictly debarred from everything that might have improved his mind or occupied his hands, had obtained permission to daub this habitation as he liked. It was octagonal, four sides being wide, four narrow; and each one was incrusted with a picture highly appropriate to the place—details of the Passion.

However, perhaps from choice, or because he had been supplied only with colour suitable to the subject and to the apartment, he had used ochre alone, merely painting monochromes, of which the tones can be imagined. After the moths had evaporated, and when my glance fell on these panels—the tints being yet more sombre in the obscurity, wherefore, in the main, I could only see the agonized attitudes and the instruments of torture without distinguishing the subject— all that men tell of *oubliettes*, and all that is known of the *san-benitos* filled my imagination. I believed firmly that these outlines were so many emblems of the fate reserved for me, and that I had been given this room solely in preparation for such a fate. I offered my life to God. Let the compassionate figure the meaning of this moment to me!

Thus housed, thus provisioned, if captives retained at least the power of talking among themselves—one known in earlier days, and not denied even to the guilty in ordinary prisons ruled by justice alone—and of seeing each other, forming such acquaintance as necessity excuses in other prisons, even between the honest man and he who is not honest—acquaintance which, in the Bastille, might often found itself on a mutual esteem; if captives retained these powers, then, without forgetting their distress, they would find a greater strength to bear it. One knows certain liqueurs which, taken separately, offend the palate; whereas mingled, the taste is less repulsive: and so it is with misfortune. This blending of sighs, however, is precisely what the Bastillors are most careful to prevent; and their pleasure would be reduced proportionately to the extent to which a prisoner might be able to temper his bitterness. Their motto is the phrase addressed by Caligula to his executioners when he ordered an assassination: " Strike in such fashion that he may feel himself die."

I have said that no prisoner was allowed either scissors, knives, or razors; therefore, when food was served to him—food soaked in his tears or repelled by his sighs—the turnkey had to slice all the pieces for him, using for this purpose a knife rounded at the end and always cautiously stowed in his pocket after the dissection.

One cannot prevent one's nails from growing, nor one's hair from sprouting; but it is not possible to get rid of these inconvenient growths without buying the privilege at the price of humiliation: the loan of scissors must be entreated and the turnkey is obliged to remain present while these are used; and he muſt remove them immediately afterward.

As to the prisoner's beard, the surgeon of the house is commissioned to shave it; a duty which he performs twice a week. He and the turnkey—agent and general superintendent of all that happens in the towers—watch carefully to see that the captive's hand does not approach the case containing the formidable inſtruments; which, like the headsman's axe, are not unwrapped until the moment for use. Everybody in the Baſtille yet remembers the uproar caused by the temerity of M. de Lally, although at that time he could scarcely foresee his deſtiny. He got possession of a razor one day, and, whilſt laughing, refused to part with it. This did not presage any especially frantic design; none the less, the tocsin sounded throughout the château. The guard was called out promptly, twenty bayonets were advancing, and perhaps cannon were being made ready, when, happily, the revolt ended by the reſtoration of the dreadful weapon to its case.

It is a mockery to pretend, as folk do, that such vigilance is direɕted as much to the safety of the gaolers as to that of the captive himself. What attack can be feared from a man loaded with chains weighted so cunningly, enclosed by so many walls, surrounded by so many guards, and isolated so scrupulously? Whatever the motive that prompts this fear of leaving such feeble means within a prisoner's reach, certainly the thing they dread is his despair. Furthermore, they know that this despair results only from the calculated torments imposed on him, and it is by sole reason of their wish to lacerate his heart with impunity that they are so anxious to take all power from his hand.

Hitherto I have spoken at some length of the turnkeys, without describing their duties. They are subordinates employed in what is called the service of

the towers, which means of the prisoners; and this
service is brief. It consists in a mere distribution of
food to each coop in an allotted department. They
come three times a day: at seven of a morning, at
eleven, and at six o'clock of an evening—the hours of
breakfast, dinner, and supper. They are watched so
that their stay shall be no longer than is necessary for
the depositing of their load. Consequently, in the
twenty-four centuries that make one day, or rather,
one night, in the Bastille, a prisoner has no more than
three short diversions.

The turnkeys are relieved even of making the beds
or of sweeping the rooms. Once more the pretext
given is that when occupied thus they might be mal-
treated, murdered, and so on. One can estimate the
worth of such motives; the practice, however, is constant.
Accordingly, an old or an infirm man, a delicate woman,
a man of letters unused to such domestic tasks or a
rich man equally unskilled—all are subjected to the
same formal code.

To say truth, the turnkeys do not always submit to
these rules: they make exceptions and sometimes give
assistance, which no one has the right to demand from
them; but this must be kept as secret as an illicit
correspondence. The Fury disguised as governor—
who takes alarm immediately he passes one of his
dungeons and cannot hear groans—would punish them
forthwith for any consolations they might have given.

To this absolute silence, this general destitution,
and, let me repeat, to a non-existence more cruel than
death—since it does not exclude pain; or, rather, it
engenders all sorts of pain—to this universal abstraction,
as I must reiterate unceasingly, they abandon a so-
called State-prisoner in the Bastille; that is to say, any
man who had displeased a minister, a clerk, or one of
their lackeys. He is abandoned without resources
of any kind, and with no distraction save his own

thoughts and apprehensions, thus to the most bitter feelings which can assail a mind unstained by crime, feelings of innocence overwhelmed, lost eternally, bereft of all chance of vindicating itself; hence he exhausts himself, fruitlessly craving the aid of the laws, the assistance of his friends, and some instruction about his supposed offence. Not only do his prayers, his groans, and his despair avail him nothing, but he knows and is told repeatedly that they are useless, this being the sole fact vouchsafed to him. At the mercy of all the horrors accompanying inactivity and tedium, horrors increased by uncertainty about his future, he feels life oozing from him day after day, likewise that he is kept alive solely in order to prolong his torture. Derision and insult unite with cruelty to swell the bitterness of miseries on which he must feed.

For example: at the end of eight months I devised a plan wherewith partly to relieve my nullity by recalling my former knowledge of geometry. I asked for a case of mathematical instruments, carefully limiting the size to three inches, so to forestall even the pretext of a refusal. I had to solicit this favour for two months: probably a council of State was necessary! However, the favour was at last accorded; the case arrived—without compasses. I protested. They answered coldly that weapons were forbidden in the Bastille.

I had to entreat anew, to supplicate, to send long memorials, solemnly discussing seriously whether there were differences between a case of mathematical instruments and a gun. Yet another month passed; then, thanks to the charity and imagination of the château commissioner, the compasses arrived. But how fashioned? . . . In bone! . . . They had ordered, and at my expense, a case of mathematical instruments, and all the parts usually made of steel were fitted with bone!

PLATE VIII

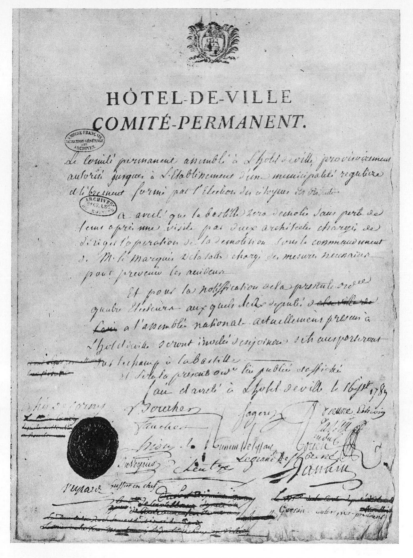

DOCUMENT RELATING TO THE DEMOLITION OF THE BASTILLE

[*face p. 208*

I preserve this original example of a geometrical outfit moſt cautiously; which, after having adorned my ſtudy during my lifetime, shall be consigned with care, and at my death, to a place where it may be displayed, figuring honourably with monuments of induſtry from uncivilized tribes, specimens occasionally brought home to us by travellers. Nowhere will any barbarous contrivance be found which merits such public curiosity.

By reason of the principle that a man committed thus into the King's, or rather the miniſter's, hands, muſt, without exception, disappear completely—and in order that this atrocious juggling may not be invalidated—matters have been arranged so that the prisoner's exiſtence shall depend exclusively on those intereſted to conceal it. The governor feeds prisoners by contraċt; and this royal cook-shop is profitable.

The miniſtry has eſtablished fifteen places at the Baſtille, which, whether occupied or otherwise, are paid for at the rate of ten French livres—or about five Brabantine florins, or eight English shillings—a day; and this brings the governor's income to upwards of 2,500 louis d'or a year.

This is not all; for when a *lettre-de-cachet* is fabricated, assigning a boarder to the governor, a sum per head is added to the original endowment, and in proportion to the prisoner's social position. Thus a peddler, a fellow of low ſtation, brings an extra half-crown a day to the common pot, *over and above the authorized ten francs* ; a bourgeois or a lawyer of inferior class, five francs; a prieſt, a financier, or an ordinary magiſtrate, ten francs; an army lieutenant, twenty-four francs; a field-marshal, thirty-six francs. I do not know what the eſtimated value of a Prince of the Blood may be in this miniſterial valuation.

Moreover, and finally, the privilege has been accorded to the governor of ſtocking his cellars with nearly a hundred casks of wine free from all dues; a

14

very considerable asset, and one which doubtless ought to guarantee and facilitate his table-supplies.

But what does he do? He sells this right to a tavern-keeper in Paris, one Joli, who pays two thousand crowns for it; and, in exchange, the governor takes the cheapest possible wine for the use of the prisoners—a wine, as may be supposed, which is nothing but vinegar. The governor considers the annual endowment of ten francs a day as part of his fixed income, for which he need render no account, and which has nothing in common with his scores; for these he uses only the excess, the extra payment, destined by the liberality of the sovereign as a supplement; furthermore, he is most careful not to use this surplus in its entirety. The details of such a subject are dishonourable; notwithstanding, they ought to be known. There are prisoners in the Bastille to whom only four ounces of meat are served at a meal. These portions have been weighed on several occasions; and the fact is known to all the inferior officers, who grumble at it. Nothing would be more easy to verify, if the inferiors who can unmask the sordid avarice of their chief could be protected from his resentment.

I admit that some tables are less meagrely supplied: mine was of this number. Is this abundance an evil or a blessing for those to whom it is accorded? I dare not decide; for, although it may be less of a humiliation, it may also conceal very dangerous snares. I know folk who lived on nothing but milk throughout the time they were in the Bastille; others, like M. de la Bourdonnaie, asked for and obtained permission to have food brought from their own houses. Such permission was invariably refused to me; nor during eight months, as I have said, was I allowed to have anything whatsoever bought for me, though I had deposited money in the hands of the château officials.

I countered this by scrupulously and cautiously

eating only a very little of each dish, and by rinsing in several changes of water everything that seemed suspicious; yet, despite these precautions, I could not avoid what I dreaded with only too much reason. On the eighth day after my arrival I was seized with fearful pains and blood-vomitings, more or less recurrent, and of which the occasional renewed attacks disclosed a return of the causes.

I have never mistaken these causes; nor have I been silent about them. A hundred times I have written to the lieutenant-general of police, saying they were poisoning me: I told his substitute by word of mouth, also the doctor, the surgeon, and the house-officers themselves; and derisive laughter was the only reply I ever received.

Those who have read older accounts will ask if prisoners are utterly deprived of air and of exercise in the Bastille; likewise those who have visited the place from curiosity—*for the curious are admitted*. The governor, though he lives outside, often comes to greet callers; and all his colleagues from the King's lieutenant to the lowest scullion can meet their friends. On gala days, on occasions when there are fireworks and illuminations, the public frequently crowd to get a good view, and they are received on the towers.

At such times these towers present nothing but an image of calm and of peace; and the strangers from outside know nothing of what takes place and is enclosed within these impenetrable vaults, of which they can admire the exterior: in fact, some of them may be trampling over the tomb of a friend, a relative—even the tomb of a father, while believing him to be two hundred leagues away, serenely occupied about his business or relishing his pleasures.

And finally, all who enjoy this external survey and observe a sufficiently large garden, and lofty platforms where, in consequence, the air is pure and the view picturesque—and who hear the assertion that such, on ordinary days, is for the use of the prisoners—leave in the persuasion that though life may not be pleasant in the Bastille, these privileges do in effect make it bearable. Possibly this may have been so in the past; but read what took place a short while ago.

The present governor, de Launey, is an ingenious man, turning all things to account; who, having determined that the garden might be made to serve a self-interested economy, rented it to a gardener. This fellow sells the fruit and vegetables, and, on that account, pays a fixed sum to de Launey each year. De Launey, however, in order to avoid constraint in this bargain, deemed it essential to exclude the prisoners from the garden; accordingly a letter, signed Amelot, was received, forbidding their use of the garden.

As to the tower platforms, though their height is so great that it would be difficult thence to recognize anyone or to be recognized therefrom, nevertheless, since they overlook the Rue Saint-Antoine, from which the public has not yet been driven, prisoners formerly were not allowed to walk there, unless escorted by one of the guardians of the château—a turnkey or an officer. Latterly, perhaps within the last three years, they discovered that this fatigue-duty was most troublesome ; in addition, conversations with the sentry resulted—and M. de Launey, in his vigilance, took alarm. Hence, partly because of his consideration for the laziness of his colleagues, partly because of his own suspicions, a letter arrived, signed Amelot, forbidding prisoners the use of the platforms, as well as of the garden.

Therefore no place remained for exercise, save the court of the château—a quadrangle about thirty-two yards by twenty yards. The surrounding walls are more than a hundred feet high, and without a single window ; thus, in reality, the court forms a deep well,

where the cold is insupportable in winter, since the
north wind is sucked down into it ; and summer heat
is equally insupportable, for the air cannot circulate,
hence the sun turns the place into a veritable furnace.
This is the sole gymnasium where those of the prisoners
to whom the privilege is granted—for it is not allowed
to all—can, turn by turn, and for a few moments each
day, disgorge themselves of the putrid air from their
dens.

Do not believe, however, that the art of persecution,
which makes the prisoner's lot so grievous, is relaxed
even during these short lapses. To begin with, the
sort of promenade afforded by such an unsheltered
place when rain falls may be imagined ; nothing but
the most vexatious weather-effects are endured here;
in addition, with the appearance of a shadow of liberty,
surrounded by sentries, in a universal silence and within
sight of the clock—the one thing allowed to break this
silence—the state of bondage is recalled all too vividly.

The château clock overlooks this court—a curious
fact! A fine clock-face is enframed; but can anybody
guess what sort of ornament and decoration has been
added to it ? Chains, perfectly sculptured! Two
figures, linked by the neck, the feet, hands, and the
middle of the body, serve as supports; and the two ends
of the ingenious garlands, having enwrapped the dial,
meet in an enormous knot; moreover, as a proof that
they menace both sexes alike, the artist, inspired by
the genius of the place—or under direct orders—has
modelled a man and a woman, and with minute care.
Such is the spectacle with which a prisoner may refresh
his vision as he promenades; and a huge inscription,
graven in letters of gold on black marble, informs him
that he owes this spectacle to M. Raymond Gualbert
de Sartine.

In 1781, during the heat making the summer of that
year memorable, I was oppressed by the atmosphere,

a vomiting of blood, and a ſtomachic weakness not provoked, yet encouraged, by the weather; nevertheless I had to pass the entire months of July and Auguſt without leaving my den, the pretext being that work was in progress on the platforms, though the workmen could have ascended from the outside; and in faɕt they did ascend thus. It was unnecessary to cross the court, except with their needful supplies of ſtone ; and this operation might have been effeɕted, as on other occasions, before nine o'clock in the morning of each day. But this seemed irksome to M. de Launey, who found it more easy to say: *No promenades !*—and there were no *promenades*.

Do not forget, in the full eſtimation of this privation, that it supplemented, and without exception, every other sort of privation with which man may be tormented; and bear in mind that not only is a prisoner thus exposed to physical perils, but to an inevitable decline in health; also, that since bodily exercise is the sole resource which, in measure, numbs the agitation of a prisoner's mind, such agitation becomes more poignant if this resource is removed; and when throughout the day he cannot even vary the anguish, his heart, surcharged with sighs, is more painfully oppressed by the walls encompassing him.

Consequently, in the prisons of normal juſtice, such harshness is considered more galling than anything otherwise permissible as a punishment for criminals under conviɕtion. Secret confinement—that is to say, absolute confinement—is only imposed during the short intervals when there is a fear that outside intercourse may supply the prisoner with information likely to promote crime. This is regulated by the situation of the premises and, in addition, by humane considerations which, usually allowing a free communication between all prisoners, only permits a deviation from rule on account of one prisoner, and this by temporarily isolating him, keeping him from reach of others as long as the reason holds for such deviation. Assuredly it is better to forbid the *promenade* to a single prisoner, rather than to deny it to all.

And now let an assertion on the subject of clothing be considered.

I was arrested, September 27th, while on my way to dine in the country; hence I wore clothes suitable to such a journey at a like season. It was utterly impossible for me to procure anything additional whatsoever in the matter of linen or of suits until the end of the following November; and during this month—one excessively cold in 1780—I had no choice but to condemn myself to remain in my room or to go naked, literally naked, to brave a promenade in the intense cold. I had money, as I have already mentioned, deposited in the hands of the officers, therefore I simply asked permission to buy breeches; which, so I was told, were presented to others.

Furthermore, toward the end of November, when at last they sent me a winter outfit from the Sieur Le Quesne, it contained stockings a child of six could not have worn; and the rest of the clothes were cut in similar proportions. Doubtless they assumed I must have grown prodigiously thin ! This will seem puerile to those alone who give no thought to the circumstances; but here is something which will not seem puerile to anyone:

I raised my voice, lamenting over such ridiculous goods; I begged the governor to return this baby-linen and to concern himself with getting something different for me, if he would not allow me to make my own purchase. He answered promptly, and in presence of his colleagues and a turnkey, that I might go and ——; that he didn't care a —— for my breeches; that either a man shouldn't act in a fashion to get himself into the Bastille, or should learn to suffer the place when he got there !

I own that his companions were ashamed, and that a week after I received a dressing-gown and breeches.

If these inconceivable atrocities were not ordered, then I must proclaim them, so to spare my successors; if they were ordered, and formed part of a treatment peculiar to me, again I must proclaim them, wherefore the conscientious governor may be assured of a recompense earned by such exactitude.

Let us now proceed to the *charitable* intentions with which D'Argenson credited the commandants of the Bastille.

From September 27th, 1780, until October, 1781— that is to say, for twelve months—I suffered not only from an absolute deprivation of all outside correspondence, or rather, from a correspondence even worse than such a deprivation, as will be seen presently; but I remained in a no less complete ignorance of everything that took place in general, or in reference to myself, no news being allowed to reach me, unless calculated to increase my despair and to rob me of hope in a future not so frightful. Much of this news —by a refinement to which one shudders to give an epithet—was false, invented solely to deceive me and to make such deception more bitter, more disastrous.

Thus, each day, I was told derisively that there could be no need to distress myself about events passing in the world, since *everybody thought I was dead* ; and they carried this jest so far as to name in detail the circumstance added by furious anger or a hideous levity to my fictitious end. They assured me that I had nothing to expect from the loyalty or the assiduity of my friends, not because, like others, they had been tricked as to my existence, but because they had betrayed me. This double imposture was intended not only to give me an unreserved confidence in the sole traitor I had actually to fear, one represented to me incessantly as my single, faithful friend; but, by the manner with which I received their insinuations, they wanted to discover whether, in effect, I had any secrets that might betray me.

In October, 1781, the Queen's confinement opened a way of hope to me. This event could not be hidden from me; for, over my head, cannon were charged to announce the news, and I could see the rejoicings evoked by it. Such events always give occasion in France for the remission even of crime-sentences; and therefore I supposed that this fact in especial might be helpful to the innocent. I wrote a brief letter to M. le Comte de Maurepas, which, since I knew his character, I had energy enough to make cheerful, almost funny. He appears to have been impressed by it; and he seemed inclined to second a public sentiment directed at last in my favour. The change in his disposition was not concealed from me; but, in order that it might not result in illusions too consoling, they took care to tell me that *he was dead*, and that he had died without doing anything for me.

Finally, in December, 1781, my constitution gave way under so many trials and misfortunes; and the physical and chemical operations which, for fifteen months, had united with moral operations to destroy my health, produced this effect. I found myself attacked to such an extent that even hope in a struggle for life now failed me; moment by moment I felt the time approaching when I should lose not so much the light invisible to me, but rather the sensibility that turned my life into the most cruel of tortures; and I wished to make a WILL. Express permission must be had for this; and I proffered a request, entreating the ministers to allow the public officer to come to me, who alone could set down my will and testament, being the only trustworthy person from whom I could gain the knowledge indispensable to avoid false dispositions.

Day by day throughout the two months endangering

me I reiterated the moſt ardent, and, I declare boldly, the moſt heartrending, entreaties on this subjeċt. The Baſtille doċtor was obliging enough personally to take to the lieutenant of police—the direċt agent of the miniſtry in such matters—a certificate as to my plight and imminent peril. A ruthless refusal was the sole answer; consequently, having been treated as if I were dead during fifteen months, and being deprived without exception of all the faculties of the living— except that of suffering—I loſt even the hope of securing the laſt rights when I should indeed have ceased to live; rights refused in no other country to the dead, certainly not to those free from the degradation of an ominous sentence.

During the paſt few years the Baſtille appears to have been the preliminary to civil suits the moſt common and, in their subjeċt and outcome, the leaſt commensurable with such a curious and dreadful beginning. It has in some sort become an antechamber to the Conciergerie.

A woman of quality is suspeċted of fabricating and of passing forged notes—and she is sent to the Baſtille.

A madman at Paris, dressed in a magiſtrate's robe, accuses a woman trading in crockery at Lyons of having been the financial confidante of a society long since defunċt—and she is sent to the Baſtille. She is released after the evaporation of this absurd suspicion, embroils herself about domeſtic affairs with some head-clerk personally intereſted in her ruin—and she is sent back to the Baſtille.

A subordinate clerk is accused of having committed forgeries in the handling of business at some great house, forgeries of a kind assuredly in no way affeċting the monarchy—and he is sent to the Baſtille.

Such was the fate of Madame de Saint-Vincent, the Demoiselle Roger, and the Sieur Le Bel. Were they

State prisoners ? What, then, was the object of the funereal system to which they were submitted ?

They were all discharged thence, to appear before ordinary judges, but, on discharge, there was no proof of their innocence; far from that, indeed, one can only believe that this innocence seemed highly problematic; for they were delivered to the expensive delays of regular justice and a considered indictment, commenced and thoroughly investigated in due form. Certainly, therefore, the evidence discovered before they were sent to judgment must have been adverse rather than favourable; thus, when they left this fatal abyss, they were more suspected than when they entered it; yet it was on their admission to the Bastille that they were overwhelmed by the system of the place! They were set free only when there was no further right to assume their guilt!* They were given a quasi-liberty when handed over to a legal trial, which, in itself, seemed to set a mark against them; a liberty entirely absent when all the accessories of the Bastille were added to such loss, and before any preliminary steps for a legal inquiry had been taken.

The system of the Bastille is instituted solely to cause pain; and pain to whom ? Admittedly to innocent men, since well-grounded suspicions lead rather to consideration and an appearance before a judge. In whose name is it instituted ? In the name of the King, of the supreme magistrate, the born protector of innocence, the guardian of the weak! It is his more direct intervention which leads to the most cruel results: his immediate orders are claimed as the authority whereby a miserable wretch—who has committed no offence against him, nor against the laws, nor against

---

* This passage in Monin's edition of Linguet's Memoirs, 1889, reads : ". . . They were set free only when there was more right to assume their guilt !"

anything respected by law—is subjected to punishments unknown in ordinary prisons, where guilty men, or men accused at least of some kind of criminal attempt, are crowded.

In the name of the King the prisoner is throttled nearly to a point of suffocation, though enough breath is spared to him so that his agony shall be endless; *in the name of the King* one scoffs at the prisoner's contortions and glories in his moans, numbering as so many victories the protracted sighs drawn from him by affliction. The King is unashamedly named as the author of these infamous prevarications, although he knows nothing of them, nor of the ministerial vengeances disavowed by his heart.

Yes! they are unknown to you! You! who were appointed by nature to be my master, whose virtues would have been my protection, if innocence had had as much right of access to the throne as calumny; you whose esteem provided the most gratifying recompense and powerful incentive to my work; you whose frank and honourable mind was not afflicted by my promise always to speak the truth, nor repelled by my exactitude in fulfilling my word!